Memoirs of a Single Travelling Mom; Travels with Toby

The adventures of a free-spirited single mom and her son as they break with conformity, travel the world, and discover their own truths.

Marnie McBain

Table of Contents

"You own everything that happened to you. Tell your stories. If people wanted you to write warmly about them, they should have behaved better."

—Anne Lamott

Chapter 1:

In the Beginning

I quickly closed the bathroom door behind me, grabbed the box out of its paper bag, and backed up onto the toilet seat. Perched there, I fumbled with the cellophane wrap, cursing. With each failed attempt, my heart pounded a little harder, my breath was becoming labored, and my muscles weak. I felt as though I was nearing the end of a marathon, exhausted but hyper at the same time.

I dropped my hands to my lap, closed my eyes, tilted my head back, and forced deep breaths. *Relax. Relax. It doesn't matter how fast or slowly you get this box open, the result will be the same.* Feeling a little less frantic, I opened my eyes and picked carefully at the cellophane. It finally ripped with a crackle. I removed the wand from the box, and unfolded the insert. It took a few moments to focus on the microscopic print.

It wasn't exactly rocket science. Pee on the wand, wait a few minutes, then count the stripes. I felt a bit silly holding the wand in the air and peeing, not only on the little test strip but everywhere else too. How to pass the minutes? Carefully placing my future in the bathroom cabinet, I closed the mirror door on it, took off my clothes, and stepped into the shower.

Warm water coursed down my body, slicking my hair to my neck and back. I stood under the waterflow with my eyes closed, thinking of something I'd read about women showering for three reasons. One: because they were dirty, two: because they needed to shave their legs and wash their hair, and three: because they needed to just stand there under the water and wait for things to pass. This was definitely the third.

Was that the door? I stepped out, shook the water from my ears, and listened.

"Hey, Marnie." Shit! Jacob! I should have locked the damned door. I wiped my face with my hands as if that would help me hear better, but didn't turn off the water. "What's this?"

I could picture him standing there, packaging in hand. "Uhh, w-what it says on the box."

"And?"

"I don't know, Jake. It's in the cabinet. You look. One stripe, I'm not; two stripes, I am." I shivered, feeling exposed, but couldn't bring myself to hide under the water again. Within seconds, the shower curtain flew open with a swoosh and clatter and Jacob, fully clothed, grinning like a loon, jumped in, picked me up, and swung me around whooping fit to disturb the neighbors.

Suddenly, he put me down and gingerly placed his hand on my still flat belly. "Sorry, I guess I need to be more careful now." The joy on his face was infectious, and I felt myself smiling back despite my fears. Tears slid down the curves of my cheeks. "Marnie?" He stepped back. "You are happy, aren't you?"

I nodded. "Tears of joy," I prevaricated. I wasn't sad, just shocked, I guess.

After my miscarriage 10 years prior, I'd been told that I would be unlikely to ever conceive again. I had been sad, not so much because I wasn't going to be a mother, but because I'd honestly thought at the time that the baby was going to save my marriage. My then husband, Will, had been devastated, not because he thought our marriage was at risk, but because he was older than me and desperate to have yet another 'thing' to add to our picture perfect life. A baby would have completed the 'Canadian Dream' for him. I obviously didn't share his sentiments because five months' later, I'd asked for a divorce. His response was to pick up the phone and call my parents saying, "I give up. Could you try and talk some sense into your daughter?"

My parents tried. They tried really hard, even going so far as to invite him to a family Christmas dinner one year after we'd split, and five months after I'd started dating a new man, Kevin (the first of a few Kevins).

Will hadn't been a bad guy. Not at all, and the guilt of leaving him weighed on me for many years. Doing 'the right thing' is so hard. I'd never really fallen in love with Will. We'd had some fun together in our early days, and our engagement was the impulsive culmination of a rather drunken and lust-filled evening. But, come morning, alongside the hangover were creeping doubts. The announcement had been made, though, and wedding plans were made quickly, too quickly. I suspect that my family was very eager to see me 'settled.' I'd always been a source of embarrassment; job hopping, dressing like a hippie, and dabbling in the spiritual. And by spiritual, I don't mean religion; that would have been welcomed. I was interested in the power of the universe, the occult, and nature, according to them, 'airy fairy' things that made no sense and were borderline evil. It didn't help either that I had strong premonitions and lived by my gut instinct.

My feelings of doubt had grown stronger with each passing day, and seven months later, the day before our wedding, my whole soul was screaming "NO!" I'd eventually burst into tears and admitted to my wedding party and mother that I didn't love Will, that I was terrified of making him miserable, and yes, selfish as it sounded, terrified of being trapped in a relationship without substance. "Don't be silly," I was told. "It's perfectly normal to have jitters the day before you get married. Every bride goes through it. It passes, and you'll look back and laugh one day. Now clean up your face and, for goodness sake, stop crying; you're going to ruin your wedding photos." So, at 24, I began four and a half years of marriage that only served to reinforce my lack of gratitude and hedonism. How could I possibly be so unappreciative of the life I'd been 'given?' We lived in our own home, I worked alongside my husband, we were on our way to fulfilling the Canadian dream; all we needed was a white picket fence and 2.5 children.

All I wanted was OUT.

That's not to say I didn't try to make things work. Of course I did. I begged for holidays, opportunities to camp out in nature, travel and spend time together. Yes, we worked together, but all that meant was that I worked for him. He did his work and I did mine. Mine was not enough to fill the day, and his consumed almost all of his waking hours. I would have liked to share the load more, giving us both some free time to be together, get to know each other and explore beyond our own little part of suburbia. Surely there was more to life than the small cities of Pickering and Markham?

Even Toronto and Canada felt insignificant in the grand scheme of things. For Will, it was not an option, and he was the boss. I guess the ambitions and yearnings of a 31-year-old businessman and a 24-year-old empath who lives by 'feeling' were really never compatible in the first place. I think that realization really hit home when, on a rare evening outing, I thoroughly embarrassed him by singing karaoke. Now that I think of it, perhaps that's why he submersed himself in work, to avoid having to deal with my 'boisterous' attempts at enjoying life in public.

I eventually started to fill my free hours with more work. I'd worked alongside my ambitious, successful mother in her condominium management business off and on since the age of 16 and obtained my accreditation as a Registered Condominium Manager shortly after completing my university degree. The logical thing to do with my lonely hours was to spend them doing part-time work for a condominium management company. It did nothing to satisfy my soul, but it did earn me some measure of approval from my family and society at large, and of course helped pay the bills. All good, right? Wrong. The accumulation of wealth was not my ambition. The accumulation of 'things' even less so. With each knickknack or piece of furniture we bought, I felt like I'd traded a small part of my soul. Every new possession was another brick slotted into my prison wall.

I digress. Out of the shower, dried, dressed, and officially pregnant, I was encouraged by Jacob's enthusiasm. Still euphoric, he said, "This is the best news. I always said we'd make great kids, and now it's happening! We've got to go out and celebrate tonight. Let's go big!"

I was swept up with his excitement and took my time getting ready, putting on light makeup, a brightly-colored 'butterfly' dress, then standing side on in front of the mirror, inspecting my full body profile. A slim, not unattractive redhead looked back. I tried to imagine the bump that would appear in a few months' time, not too sexy. I quelled that little inner voice that kept reminding me that by the time I was five months' pregnant, I'd have been pregnant for more than half of our relationship. Not to mention that, in two days' time, I'd be turning 38. I put a smile on my face and told the inner voice to shut up. We were going to do it right. Yes, I was still in party mode. I'd never seemed to get out of it after leaving Will; after all, I was making up for lost time and I dreaded the thought of giving up alcohol—would those parties be as much fun without it? But, if I was going to have this child, I wasn't going to let it be born with fetal alcohol syndrome.

Okay, I rationalized, there were going to be sacrifices, but that was okay. I might not like it, but I could do it. I'd managed to do things I didn't like doing all my life, and for 'other' people. This was different; this would be for my son. Son? I looked at myself quizzically in the mirror. How did I know that? I don't know. I just did.

The restaurant was bright and cheery, but stylish. So was Jacob. I looked at him over the table, so gorgeous. Our child would benefit from looking like his dad. I felt an odd disconnect. Jacob didn't look like a dad. I batted the thought aside. I, with my tattoos and piercings, should be the last one to judge! I smiled at the irony. Maybe it was just because Jacob was still in his twenties. Late twenties, admittedly, but suddenly that previously irrelevant little age gap seemed to have stretched. I pulled myself back into celebration mode and smiled broadly at Jacob.

"You're the best, sexiest sugar momma, Marnie, and now you're going to be the best, sexiest mom!" Jacob laughed. My stomach clenched and the smile on my face froze. It wasn't the first time he'd referred to me as his sugar momma, but somehow this time, I couldn't laugh, and there was no witty comeback; it was all I could do to keep that smile going. I gave myself a mental shake and dug deep to find that little bubble of excitement that I'd felt earlier, that optimism. I found the optimism, albeit a thinner, less robust version, but the excitement was nowhere to be found. Maybe it would be back later.

While I hadn't been desperate for a child with my first pregnancy, we'd been trying, and I was very sad when I'd spent my 4th wedding anniversary in the hospital having the medical staff finish what nature had seen fit to start but not complete. This pregnancy was totally unexpected, and the discovery was only a few hours old. I'd grow into it.

At the end of the meal, the waitress arrived at the table. "You all have a good meal?" she asked, presenting the bill to Jacob. We both smiled and said yes. It had been good. The food was great. I wasn't completely sure about my frame of mind, I was all over the place, but that wasn't the restaurant's fault. "Glad to hear it, I'll be back in a sec," she said, beaming at Jacob before moving to another table. I smiled at Jacob, and he smiled back, a charming grin.

"Do you mind…?" he said, passing the bill over to me. The lights seemed to flicker a little and dim. I looked around. Nobody else seemed to have noticed. Jacob was still smiling, his hand outstretched. *Actually, I do mind!* The words were loud and clear in my head, but my mouth stayed closed. All my doubts gathered and congealed, heavy and cold in my stomach. I shook my head, unable to trust my voice, and took the bill from him. It wasn't that I thought men should always pay. I usually paid when we went out; Jacob was useless at budgeting, and his salary rarely made it to month's end. Our living arrangement was that he would contribute fifty percent to household expenses, which he'd never done. But just this once? Couldn't he spring for his baby's incubator? It was a quick flare of annoyance and just as quickly suppressed, but it took root in the lump of congealed doubt. It made me think about diapers and the myriad other things that babies need. Midnight feeds, etc. and I wondered whether these too were to be my sole responsibilities. A bit late, I realize. But it wasn't as if I had thought I might fall pregnant. Anyway, now that I was, I was going to make the best of it.

The next day, I woke and stretched, then remembered the little life growing inconspicuously inside of me. I smiled and went to the bathroom to talk to this new being without disturbing Jake. "Hello there," I whispered. "Don't stress, my boy, I'm just a little confused right now, but we'll get this figured out. I'm not going to let you grow up feeling unwanted. If you are born, I'll do what I can to make you happy." A little wave of self-pity stung the back of my eyes. I analyzed it cautiously. Was I feeling sorry for myself because I was pregnant? No. It wasn't that. Was I scared of losing this baby? No, I somehow knew this one was here to stay. Because I feared I might end up being a single mom? No, not really. Had I felt unwanted? No. Had I felt unloved? Kind of, yes. I know I'm not 'unloved' in its strictest sense; I know that my parents love me, they demonstrated it numerous times. I think right then, though, considering this unborn child and the unconditional love I felt was his due, I was reminded of all the times that I had been accused of disappointing others, be it my parents, my brother and his family, or my ex-husband. Feeling like a disappointment somehow always took the shine off love for me, like I was no longer deserving of it. I had to be a certain way to earn that love. I frequently failed to live up to the standards of others. I wasn't going to disappoint this child, and I wasn't going to make him feel like a disappointment. I smiled again; clearly, maternal instincts were setting in already.

I hoped the whole unconditional love thing wouldn't be too hard. It had certainly been really easy to disappoint in the past. All I'd had to do was be true to myself—that simple. I thought of my marriage and how shocked family and friends had been by my divorce. Why? I had warned them going into it that I didn't think it would work. Despite my best efforts, I'd felt so unworthy, such a failure, and when I eventually threw in the towel, the guilt was all mine. I knew that I was blamed. After all, Will had given me so much. What more could a woman want? The problem was I hadn't wanted more, not materially. I'd have settled for far less. I wanted life beyond the office and house. I wanted to be me, to be allowed to express my own personality, belt out karaoke, camp under the stars, dress the way I felt comfortable, and read and talk about what interested me without worrying about what the neighbors thought. Geez, I thought, it must be pregnancy hormones. I hadn't thought about my botched marriage this much in a couple of years.

I pulled myself together. Enough. I'd been accused of running away from my 'problems' when I'd left Will, and again when I'd moved out of town to take some of the pressure off my family. "I'm not always running away," I told the little life inside of me. "I'm running towards me. I think I'm being brave. I'm trying to live life on my terms, and it shouldn't affect anyone else. I need to feel free to be me." I paused. "I hope you're going to like me."

I went about my morning in much the same way as I had before those two little stripes had appeared on the wand. There was something vaguely surprising about the way daily rituals continued undisturbed, watching my hands physically executing tasks like an automaton, while my mind was focussed only on this new life. I would eventually have to call my parents and let them know. I hoped they'd be happy for me. If not for me, then for themselves; they were finally getting a grandson after all. What was that meme I'd seen the other day? Something about grandchildren being the reward for gritting your teeth and not strangling your children during their teenage years? That brought the smile back again. After having gritted their teeth so hard they probably needed dental surgery, it must have been a terrible disappointment when I'd failed to carry my baby to term and robbed them of that reward, from me anyway.

By the time I got around to making the call, I'd found that little bubble of excitement I'd been looking for the previous night. Nerves made my hands shake a little, but it was an excited nervousness. I laughed at myself. Imagine feeling nervous. I was 38, totally self-sufficient, and about to deliver the news of a miracle, a gift of life. The reward they thought they'd never get. I'd be settling that debt for putting them through my teenage years of angst and 'drama'—whenever I'd heard my name from an adult mouth, the word 'drama' usually followed not long thereafter. Maybe not always in the same sentence, but very often in the same paragraph, or as soon as I left the room and they thought I was out of earshot. I'd started thinking of it as my middle name.

I'd procrastinated enough. Drunk water, gone to the toilet, splashed my face with water. It was time. I dialed and waited, listening to the ringing and imagining my mom crossing the room to answer. "Hellooo." She always sounded happy when she answered the phone in her sing-song 'phone voice.'

"Hi, Mom, it's me."

"Marnie?"

"Yeah."

"What's wrong?" The happy tone of her voice was replaced with concern. Why was it that so often when she heard from me, she thought there was a problem? I rubbed my free hand against the seam of my jeans.

"Nothing. Actually, I've got some good news. I'm pregnant. I'm having a baby!" Long silence. I tried to picture her facial expression, but couldn't.

"Oh my God, Marnie, you're not married—how did this happen? What are you going to do now? You are going to get married now, right?"

The conversation deteriorated from there, and by the time I'd disconnected the call, I was in no doubt as to the new level of disappointment to which I'd sunk. I don't know why I felt as shocked as I did. The last thing on my mind had been what 'everyone' would think of me. I was completely wrapped up in my own confusion about how to cope with an unplanned baby, and wonder at the fact that I could in fact have a baby. I felt like a cat that had just proudly and lovingly presented its owner with the precious gift of…a dead rat.

I curled up tight in the chair next to the telephone and obsessed. I'd been stupid to just break the news the way I did. I should have realized that it was going to be more of a shameful thing than a celebration. I was just so stupid. Would I never learn? I thought of the time I'd gone to a clinic in my teens when I became sexually active. I'd sat in the waiting room on my own, waiting to be seen and to ask for 'The Pill.' My mind wrestled with pride and guilt. Pride that I was actually taking such a big adult step on my own, and guilt that I hadn't told my parents what I was up to. While this debate twisted and squirmed in my mind, a girl my age had come into the room with her mother. I'd tried to still my mind and eavesdrop on their conversation.

They chatted in a relaxed manner about life, birth control, and her boyfriend. I envied them the closeness of their relationship. They were so perfectly in tune.

Guilt won. I should have given Mom the opportunity to have that sort of relationship with me. I was denying her and myself. What an idiot. I started to fantasize about the conversation I'd have when I got home. We would bond over this; after all, she and my dad had eloped when her parents wouldn't give their consent to marry. She was a 'woman of the world,' a strong female with a mind and will of her own. This big step in my life was the perfect opportunity to connect.

I'd rushed home in excitement, and waited agitatedly for a moment when she would be finished with her clients and my father was not around, so that I could tell her about this next wondrous phase of my life. I was looking forward to a cosy chat and heaps of advice. I couldn't have been more wrong. My mother, far from making us coffee and sitting at the kitchen table to dispense wisdom with a beatific smile, nearly collapsed in horror. "Marnie! How can you do this to us? You seem hellbent on bringing shame on this family! People will have seen you there; it's bad enough that you're promiscuous without publicising it. Everyone is going to be calling you a slut."

Slut! It stung like a slap. It sucked me back a few years to when I'd had my first boyfriend. I was about 12, and obviously an early bloomer because none of my classmates were dating yet. Funny that, because now it's the norm. But not then. It had been the beginning of my realization that I was 'different.' I hadn't had many friends at school, and those that I had were not very close. I was too busy trying to figure out the meaning of life, reading about psychic powers, and exploring the world of Wicca while they were more focused on fashion and music. Don't get me wrong, I loved music too, but Blondie, Dolly Parton, and Kim Carnes were not my scene. I rocked to Pink Floyd's *The Wall*. I also loved clothes, but I was more interested in color and comfort than what was in and what wasn't. My lack of appreciation for the latest styles and trends meant that I was 'out' far more often that I was 'in.'

It was hardly the world's greatest love affair; we were both 12 and I can't even recall how we met. Brian was from the other side of town, both literally and figuratively; about an hour's travel by public transport. I liked a lot of things about him. I liked the fact that he wasn't afraid to express his opinions and that those opinions were often controversial. I thought he was so brave. He was a bit of a rebel and my role model. But probably even more than that, I liked the title of 'girlfriend.' It made me feel so grown up. I belonged. He had chosen me. Someone who had the courage to be himself thought I was worth the hour's travel. I felt special.

Whether it was jealousy, spite, or just a typical schoolgirl need to all be equal, my relationship attracted a lot of unwelcome attention at school. I can still see myself walking home from school, crossing the road to avoid a group of staring, whispering girls. As I passed, their faces screwed up with what I can only describe as hate. I pretended I couldn't hear, but the word "SLUT!" screamed across the expanse of the road reached me, slapped me, and burnt itself permanently into my brain. I didn't always pretend I didn't hear; as things got worse, there were often times that I responded angrily, accusing them (just as loudly) of jealousy because they couldn't get a boyfriend if they tried. I thought I was fighting bravely for my honor and my relationship. What I was actually doing was increasing the size of the target on my back.

The worse the name-calling got, the more important Brian became in my life. I needed to defend him. I needed to defend us. I started dreading going to school. My parents, concerned, spoke to the school counsellors; initially, my behavior was put down to being a teenager and acting out, as teenagers do. Later, this was diagnosed as depression. It culminated in a suicide attempt in grade 9. But that's not a subject for now. The relationship for which I'd fought so hard was not worth it anyway. It ended abruptly in a blaze of humiliation and horror when I found him in a cemetery having sex with a girl from his school. I was shattered. Betrayed. And angry. Very angry.

I was disillusioned with 'men.' My heart and reputation were in tatters, and I was the slut? The epithet stuck and became something of a self-fulfilling prophecy. My young self thought, well if the hat fits… I wouldn't go so far as to say that I actually became a 'slut'—I still can't bear that word. But I didn't let myself care so much about what people thought. It didn't seem I was ever going to outgrow the label; there was no reputation left to protect. I was already condemned. This didn't endear me to my peers, or my family. In a somewhat bizarre way, it lifted some of the pressure off me. Not that the lack of pressure brought happiness. I drifted from one unfulfilling relationship to another, every single one of them ruined by my partner's infidelity.

I uncurled from my fetal position in the chair and placed my hand on my stomach. "Okay, Sunshine. That didn't go too well," I murmured. "It looks like it's just going to be you, me, and Dad." Famous last words.

That night, Jacob and I went out again. Still celebrating. The evening felt very long without alcohol. Funny how time flies when you're a participant and it drags so slowly when you're just an observer. Jacob and 'our' friends drank toast after toast to his pending fatherhood. Some of the toasts earlier in the evening were quite funny. They were a witty bunch. The later it got, though, the more outrageous and personal the toasts grew. To a point where they were revelling in hilarity while I looked on and smouldered. This wasn't a joke. We were having a baby, and I was tired. I'd become the grinch. I tried a couple of times to suggest that we go home, but to no effect. Eventually, I resigned myself to drinking soft drinks and watching the goon show.

In the car on the way home, I was smarting. This was only day two. The future wasn't looking too rosy. I decided I needed more buy-in from Jacob, and that honesty was the best policy. "Jake, do you think you could help me with the not drinking thing?"

"Sure thing. No problem. I thought you did well tonight, though. You didn't have any booze, did you?" He glanced at me.

"No. No, I didn't. But I was thinking, maybe we could give up together; it would be easier if we're both in the same boat."

He laughed uproariously. "We're not in the same boat. I didn't get myself knocked up! Why should I be punished?" Silence. He repeated it again, bellowing with laughter at his alcohol-sharpened wit. Silence. "What now?" He shot me a petulant look. "Don't tell me you've lost your sense of humor?" I had. "Oh, for fuck's sake." We drove home in mutual mute indignation, slammed a few doors, and went to bed without saying another word.

The next morning, my 38th birthday, I woke feeling miserable. It was clear that my life was on the threshold of permanent change and Jacob's was not. On a conscious level, I realized that for the first time, I was actually hoping for the white picket fence. Not so much for me, but for my baby. Something had fractured last night; the life inside me had stopped being 'ours' and become 'mine.' On a subconscious level (that feeling in my gut, that has proved to be my most reliable source of direction), I knew that it wasn't going to happen. Somewhere in there, buried under a mound of conscious objections, was a bit of information that I'd been deliberately ignoring for some time. Jacob was in love with the idea of being in love. Worse than that, from the number of times he mentioned her in conversation, I had a sneaking suspicion that if he was in love with anyone, it was his ex, Sarah, and not me.

Jacob obviously felt that it wouldn't be 'right' to sulk through my birthday. So, he wished me a happy birthday and suggested that we go out for dinner to celebrate. I was feeling a bit done with celebrations, but it would be churlish for me to reject his olive branch. So, we went.

My heart sank when he passed me the bill at the end of the meal again with his charming smile. We had avoided any contentious subjects during dinner, and I appreciated his effort, so I paid, again, without saying a word. Happy birthday to me. We'd managed to get through the day without resurrecting last night's argument, and I was grateful for small mercies. As we pushed our chairs back and stood, Jacob said, "Right, where to next?"

"Home," I responded.

"Don't be ridiculous. It's your birthday. Let's go get a drink."

"I'm not drinking, remember?"

"For God's sake, Marnie! Are you the only person that matters in your life?"

"Actually, no, Jake. I'm not. There are two of us; I'm pregnant now, remember? I have to think about my baby too."

"Exactly. It's all about YOU and YOUR baby. You're going to be pregnant for NINE months! Do you honestly expect me to sit at home and watch you 'be pregnant' for the next NINE months?"

"No. No, I don't, but we've been out three nights in a row, and I don't see the need to go drinking right now. I'm tired."

"Oh God! Me, myself, and I. I'm sick of it!"

"Jacob!" I was stung by the unfairness of it all. "This is our new reality. Our lifestyle has to change to allow for this baby."

"It's not 'our' new reality, Marnie. It's YOURS! Don't suck me into it. I'm not putting my life on hold while you wallow in YOUR pregnancy." We drove home in taut silence yet again.

We barely spoke over the next few days; this gave me lots of time to think. Maybe too much time. I felt so confused. Eventually, I told Jacob that I was going to go to Mexico for a week, to think about our relationship on my own. He looked relieved to see me go. I spent a full week thinking. I even thought about whether or not to keep my baby. Yes, I actually thought very briefly about ending the pregnancy. I meditated and took long walks alone on the beach. I focused on connecting with the little nugget of sunshine growing inside of me. I even spoke to 'Sunshine' from time to time, but never could bring myself to tell him everything that was on my mind.

How could I? But almost as though he sensed my indecision, I started dreaming of him at night. I had a dream in which I was standing in front of a pyramid in Egypt alongside a little blond boy. It became a recurring dream.

Within a few days, I realized there was no way I could even contemplate ending my pregnancy. I felt as though my baby was communing with me, begging me to commit to him. Somehow, his voice came through loud and clear, and our spirits connected. It's hard to explain. It's not that I heard an 'actual voice,' but I 'heard' him, mentally, asking me to, for once, not walk or run away from my problems. I took stock. I'd run away so often, avoided confrontation, escaped from situations. But he was not a situation, nor was he a choice. He was the beginning of an unspoiled human being, who deserved to be born, and he needed me. Flying back to Canada, I made that commitment. I would be there for him. Always. I would also make a concerted effort with Jake. I would not run away or shut him out whenever things became uncomfortable. I was completely committed to our baby and our life together. Together, we could do this.

Chapter 2:

Possession is Nine-Tenths of

the Law

It was such a relief to be home, to have made a decision and committed to our baby and life together. I knew it wouldn't be easy, but I was feeling strong, and I believed that love and determination were all it would take. I could do this. Our baby was going to have a stable family life filled with unconditional love. I couldn't wait to tell Jacob, and to explain that, although financial support would be welcome, what we really needed was for him to support us in other ways. By being there, and being understanding of the changes that I needed to go through in order to give our baby a solid start in life.

My buoyed mood faltered as I entered my home; it was a trainwreck. Clothes on the floor, two wet towels in the bedroom—one on the unmade bed, and dirty dishes in the sink. Empty beer cans everywhere; on the coffee table, the arm of the couch, and lying on the floor. I unpacked my bags, then started on the big clean up. I was not going to get angry. This was my first test, and I was going to pass it.

By the time Jacob got home from work, things were looking more normal. Normal in my house wasn't picture perfect, but at least relatively tidy. The house always looked 'lived-in,' but it was clean. I felt like a schoolgirl, waiting nervously for Jacob to get back. But I was excited too. I was going to tell him that all was forgiven and that we could make this work. Actually, nix that, telling him that all was forgiven wouldn't go down well. It would start an argument about who owed who forgiveness. I would just tell him that I was willing to put in a big effort to make this work.

"We can do this, Jake. I know we can." I was trying to sound optimistic and upbeat, but feeling a bit ashamed at the pleading sound in my voice.

"Of course we can," he responded. "It'll just mean a bit of give-and-take."

"Exactly."

We smiled at each other and leaned in for a kiss. Perfect.

The next morning, we left for work together. At the car, I stopped short. "Jacob, what happened here?" I tried to keep the pitch of my voice low and calm as I surveyed the scratches across the roof of my car.

"What...where?" His face and voice were the picture of innocence.

"Here, Jacob. These marks on the roof."

"'Dunno. I never noticed those before."

"It looks like someone slid something hard across it...like a beer case."

"Oh, yes. It could be. I gave Mike a lift to the bottle shop. He might have put his case on the roof."

"Was he driving my car?"

"No, of course not."

"Then why would he have put the case on the roof on the driver's side?"

"Marnie." I heard the warning tone in his voice. "Don't start. We're supposed to be working on this relationship. The Spanish inquisition isn't a good way to get it going."

I got in the car and winced as I closed the door with a bang; I'd tried to be gentle. I took a deep breath while he walked around and climbed in on the passenger side. At the first downhill, there was a clatter and waft of stale beer as a stash of empty cans rolled out from under my seat.

I took a deep breath and asked, "Could you pick those up?"

He muttered under his breath as he leaned over to collect the cans. The only phrase I caught was, "Mother Theresa."

"I'm not complaining," I defended myself. "It's a safety issue; you can't drive a car with cans rattling around. What if one got stuck under the brake pedal?" I flushed at my own perversion of the truth. My stomach was boiling with rage and I felt like a wimp for pretending it was okay that he drove my car while drinking and scratched the roof. The pathetic whine to my voice disgusted me. We drove on in silence, me wrestling with feelings of disgust, anger, and guilt that I was already struggling with this new give-and-take relationship. I couldn't help but suspect that I'd be doing the giving and he'd be doing the taking. Thinking that way just intensified the guilt. I had to try harder.

Week one of happy family wasn't going well. I tried not to be angry as friends from various clubs in Red Deer told me about how much booze-fuelled fun Jacob had been having while I was in Mexico. I managed to keep a lid on it until one friend told me that she'd seen Jacob out with another woman, and had actually seen them clinched in a hot embrace, faces glued together. I lost it.

"I can't believe that you would cheat on me while I'm pregnant and while we're trying to create a future for our child!" I yelled, all sense of decorum out the window.

"And I can't believe that you believe everyone except me!" He bellowed back. "You had the gall to just push off to Mexico and lick your wounds. What did you think I was going to do? Sit here and wait for you to come back and hand me YOUR decision? Everything's always about you, isn't it? Now you come waltzing back, crap on me for everything under the sun, believe every story you hear, and expect me to be grateful for your efforts? I'm not your servant, Marnie. I'm not going to live my life according to your rules. Fuck you!"

I felt physically winded for a moment, then all the pent-up anger detonated. I screamed and shouted like a banshee. I can't even remember all the words I used, but suffice it to say, I used language that I'd never use in front of my mother. Vitriol flew. Just before he left with a slam of the back door that reverberated through the neighborhood, I was screaming, "Get out! Just get the fuck out of my house!"

I felt sick with anger. I felt even sicker that our Sunshine would have heard everything that went down. I sat on the floor cradling my stomach and apologizing to our baby between outbursts of tears. What a mess.

It was almost a week before Jacob returned. A week in which he stayed with his mate Jared, when he was home. I took to sneaking by their house at odd hours to check if his car was there. On a few nights, it was out all night. On one occasion, I saw him and Jared piling drunk out of the car with two equally drunk women in the early hours of the morning. I saw him at work, but we didn't speak. I berated myself for having mishandled things so badly. What a failure; even as a pregnant 38-year-old I was incapable of holding a relationship together. I have never felt so alone, or so repulsed by my self-pity.

He returned just before Valentine's day. We talked things through, cried and hugged, and ended up in bed together. We agreed that I would not refer to 'my' house or 'my' baby. I would not tell him to get out of what he considered his own home. It was emasculating and unfair. On the evening of the 14th, he didn't come home. I sat alone; my feelings of abandonment intensified by the fact that most other people would be celebrating their love while I had no idea where he was. All my calls went unanswered.

The next day, he was at work. I didn't say anything, but the tension was thick. Eventually, at lunch time, he came over to me and said, "I'm sorry, I just needed to be by myself."

I nodded. "It's okay, I understand." I didn't. I was turning into a liar.

We didn't refer to the incident for a couple of days, until I heard that he'd spent Valentine's night with his ex, Sarah. I couldn't do this anymore. I needed him gone. But I was scared. I knew he was going to be wild. Jacob didn't take rejection well, and I'd promised not to throw him out. I spent most of the day planning how best to broach the subject. I planned speeches, considered his possible responses, and how to deal with them. The pending fight grew out of all proportion in my mind. It consumed me.

By that evening, I thought I had covered all the bases. I even carried a small recorder in my pocket so that if he ever tried to weasel his way back into my life, I could replay the fight and remind myself why I couldn't allow it. It was every bit as bad as I'd imagined it would be. The fight was hateful, with terrible accusations flying from both sides. I don't need to listen to the recording to remember some of the awful name-calling, or to remind myself that he threatened to hit me. I was appalled by the thought that this could affect my unborn baby. Yes, mine. As of that day, I realized that this baby was mine and mine alone. Jacob didn't want me or my child if it meant that he was going to need to change his lifestyle of late-night partying and womanising. As much as he'd thought it'd be fun to have a baby, we were an inconvenience. I was not going to let my child grow up feeling like a tiresome intruder. I wanted him to be proud of who and what he is, and not apologetic for the 'disruption' caused by his existence. I was going to raise him to feel loved and appreciated.

I wish I could say that this was my epiphany, my transition to motherhood and all things maternal. It wasn't. It was a small start of thinking in the right direction, but it wasn't constant, nor was it powered by strength. It was a weak flickering flashlight with dying batteries. I was plagued by doubts. My parents were humiliated by my pregnancy and withdrawn. My brother James' live-in partner had discovered that she was pregnant a week after I had, and the congratulations were streaming in on Facebook. My parents were excited to become grandparents—of James and Karen's child. The subject of my pregnancy was taboo. I have never felt as alone as I did then. I cried for myself and my baby. I bristled with anger at the thought that one 'out of wedlock' pregnancy was a wondrous achievement, yet another milestone obligingly ticked off the list, and mine was cringeworthy.

I sank into a horrible depression. I barely slept at night. My mind replayed fights with Jacob and censure from my parents. The feeling of failure grew, and grew. I couldn't even hold a relationship together. I'd failed at childhood, been a major disappointment to my family; how could I possibly think that I could parent a helpless baby? My mind niggled constantly at the subject, like a tongue unable to stop working at a newly chipped tooth. It was exhausting. I teetered on a fine edge between guilt and anger. Sometimes I was angry at my family, sometimes at Jacob, and often at myself.

It became clear to me that I was not worthy of this child. I didn't know what to do. I had bonded with him and didn't know how I would ever be able to live with myself if I aborted him. If I thought Jacob's temper amounted to abuse, what would 'getting rid of' my baby be. Murder? I couldn't give birth to him and hand him over to Jacob. Not after I'd seen Jacob's lack of interest in stepping up to the plate and his booze-filled rages. I also suspected that he might be abusing other substances, and after his physical threat, I worried for my child. Would I be able to give him up for adoption? I wept at the thought, imagining him growing up wondering why nobody wanted him. What if he ended up being sent from foster home to foster home? I wept softly at the thought of this imaginary rejection of an innocent child. "I do want you, Sunshine," I murmured to my belly. "But how the hell am I going to take care of you? I'm a complete failure. I don't even deserve to live." I was crying openly now. Big ugly sobs. I hated myself for having started something that I couldn't finish. For creating a life when I didn't even know how to live my own without upsetting everyone around me. I wanted to die.

I could hear myself crying. Howling. The anguish both physical and mental; my chest and stomach hurt. I was short of breath. My whole body shuddered as I gasped for air, choking on my own saliva. I was drowning in sorrow. I was grieving. My hands couldn't keep still; I shoved them through my hair, wiped my sweaty face, clawed at my cheeks, slammed my fist onto the table, tore at my clothes and my skin. My arms stung where my nails had raked at them, but it wasn't enough; I needed to inflict pain on myself, punish myself for being so stupid, so inconsiderate, and such a complete and utter failure. I deserved to die.

That's it! I knew what I had to do. I pushed my chair back from the table, leaving it lying where it clattered to the floor. I snatched my car keys from the hook in the kitchen and fled to the garage. Inside, I closed the garage door, and flung myself into the driver's seat. I opened all four windows, and started the vehicle. I sat numbly, waiting for the fumes from the exhaust to envelope me, to take me away from all this pain. I imagined Jacob finding out that I was dead. I pictured him saying, "Good riddance, stupid bitch." His face was angry. I envisioned my parents. My mother crying, my father comforting her. My brother saying to them, "What did you expect? She's been a disaster waiting to happen since she was born. I would never do that to you. God, she's so selfish!"

My head throbbed, and I felt like I was listing to the left, like a sinking ship. I rolled my head to the left, and rested it against the door. It was heavy, very heavy. My neck couldn't support it anymore. My stomach churned uncomfortably. I closed my eyes. Then I heard it. A small voice. "Mommy, no. Please, Mommy, don't."

"I'm sorry, Sunshine. So sorry." My words were slightly slurred.

"I *NEED* you, Mommy, *please!*"

I jolted alert. My body was sluggish, and my brain was fumbling, trying to make sense of half thoughts that drifted and bounced off each other. Oh God! What was I doing? I reached forward, my arm weighty and slow, my movements uncoordinated. I turned the key to the off position and dragged myself out of the car. My legs couldn't hold me and I slid to the ground. On my hands and knees, I reached the garage door, stopping to retch. Then crawling on. I managed to pull the door up a gap, but couldn't get it to go higher; it seemed to weigh a ton. Eventually, I wriggled out from under the slightly open door, grazing my back on the base of the door as I went. Outside now, I threw up on the grass. My throat burned. I lay for a while until the grass against my cheek itched and I opened my eyes. Oh God. The sun was beating down.

I dragged myself to the house and leaned against the coolness of the wall. I tried to walk to the bathroom, but collapsed back onto the floor, pain shooting up my right knee as I landed on all fours. I crawled to the bathroom. The same bathroom where I'd discovered my pregnancy. I hung my head over the toilet bowl and vomited until I was completely empty. Even then, my body continued to heave, great, dry muscular spasms. It felt as though I might turn inside out at any minute. Drained, I fell asleep on the floor, my cheek pressed against the cold porcelain toilet stand.

My first confused thought on waking was that I'd been drunk and passed out. Then it hit me. I'd tried to kill myself. And my baby. Oh God! Sunshine. Bitter tears stung my eyes and my throat tightened. I sobbed. I wanted my mom. I staggered to the bed, lay down, and closed my eyes. Maybe I would still die.

My body was sluggish, and my eyes struggled to stay open. I don't know how long I slept; one day ran into another as I drifted from wakefulness to sleep and back again. In total, I spent five days in bed. Every time I awoke, it was a rude reminder that I wasn't dead.

I cried a lot. I was crying for my baby. I needed to know if he had survived, but he was too small for there to be any active signs. My stomach was still flat and I wouldn't have been able to feel any movement yet even if he was still alive. I wanted my mom. Eventually, I got up, stumbled through to the kitchen, and poured a glass of water. My mouth was dry and my throat tender; it felt like it stuck together momentarily every time I swallowed. My tongue felt almost swollen. The water was cool, sweet, and soothing. I sat on the chair next to the telephone and fantasized about calling my mother. I couldn't do that. She'd be so hurt, and angry. My father? No. I couldn't do it to him either. My brother? Definitely not. He would roll his eyes and accuse me of attention seeking and having no concern for anyone else. My family would feel hurt and unhappy, and it would all be my fault. I couldn't tell anybody. I couldn't ask for help without dragging others down, sucking them into the drama that was my sick, sordid, pathetic life.

My throat swelled and tightened and a tear slid from the corner of my eye to my chin. I dashed it away angrily. Selfish. Self-indulgent. I hated self-pity. Being called sorry for myself hurt almost as much as being called a slut. It was another label that I couldn't shake. I was just about to castigate myself for being so maudlin and wallowing in my own misery when a thought suddenly struck me. If my baby was dead, my body would have at least made an attempt at expelling it. I thought of my miscarriage. While I'd had to have a D and C, there had been initial bleeding. That's how I'd known that something was wrong. I staggered to the bathroom and yanked down my panties. They were clean!

Once again, I was perched on the toilet, shaking. This time, with excitement. I knew it. I knew in my gut that Sunshine was alive. I was being given a second chance. No more messing up! I dropped my head into my hands and cried again. Silent tears of relief. I had almost made the biggest mistake of my life. "Please forgive me, Sunshine. Please forgive me. I'm going to love you forever. I will never hurt you. I promise you. Trust me on this. I will always be there for you." I was alone in the house, and I started to laugh at myself for having wasted time running to the bathroom to check my underwear. There would have been nobody there to be offended if I'd just dropped my drawers in the living room. "Oh, Sunshine. Your mother is an idiot. But we can do this, okay? Together, we can do this. We're a team." I wiped the tears from my face. We were going to be okay.

I returned to work for a few more months after my 'sick leave,' waiting for my maternity benefits to kick in. I would receive a year's worth, at 60% of my salary. Without the expense of picking up the tab for Jacob, we could survive; and I was frugal. I had some savings. I felt confident that we would be okay. As a plumber, Jacob worked onsite most of the time, so I was spared the daily strain of having to interact with him. My stomach did clench when his name came up on the payroll, and I had to resist the urge to 'forget' a zero on his payslip. On the occasions that I did see him, he studiously ignored me. I did the same. It looked easier for him than it felt for me. He was the father of my child.

Eventually, 5 months into my pregnancy, it was time for me to take leave and focus on preparing for Sunshine's arrival. I tidied my house a lot. It was starting to look positively homely. Then, when there was no more tidying to do, I started to imagine the future. I read up on diapers, breastfeeding, and anything else 'baby' I could find. When they start talking, walking, getting teeth etc. I bought magazines. I was studying for the most important exam of my life. I started investigating all the equipment and paraphernalia that was needed to welcome a baby into the world. It was a lot more than I'd thought, and a lot more expensive than I'd thought.

Chatting to a friend one day, she said, "I can't understand why you don't want to ask Jacob to help you?"

"Because. We're not talking."

"Well, that's just silly. Why should your child suffer because his parents are stubborn? I'm sure that if you just put your pride in your pocket and spoke to him, he'd be reasonable."

"I don't know. I kind of don't want to feel beholden to him. And I don't want to open the door to letting him back in."

"Don't worry about that. I don't think that's on his agenda. He's back with Sarah. Well, sort of."

"What do you mean sort of?" I was annoyed with myself for feeling sad about him reuniting with Sarah; after all, it wasn't as if I wanted him back. I needed to grow up and be happy; okay, maybe not happy, but relieved that he had moved on.

She shrugged. "You know Jacob. He's back with Sarah, but seeing someone else on the side. Anyway," she continued, "this isn't about you, or Jacob. It's about your baby. Your child deserves to be supported by two parents. Don't be pigheaded about it."

After that conversation, I started to think about how it might be nice for our baby to have the support of two parents, even if we couldn't live together. How having two sets of grandparents would be better than one. I imagined Jacob's mom getting as excited about this birth as my parents were about Karen's pregnancy. Jacob had a twin sister, and her children would be Sunshine's cousins; he shouldn't be missing out on all that love. Maybe that was it. Maybe it was easier to be non-judgemental of your grandchild's mother if she wasn't your child. Maybe he could have some kind of extended happy family after all.

I toyed with the idea a lot. I was wary of getting drawn back into Jacob's web, though, or getting into another fight. Eventually, I decided to leave the decision to the universe. I wouldn't make it, and I wouldn't beg. I would approach Jacob about child support. If he agreed, then I'd know he was seriously interested in being part of our child's life, and I would make a concerted effort to involve him and his mom. If he refused, then I would know that he was not and I would cut him out of my life completely.

Unwilling to face a big emotional scene, I took the coward's way out and phoned him.

"Hello." His voice was so familiar, it felt funny talking to him on the phone.

"Um, Jake, it's Marnie..."

"What do you want?"

"That's not nice."

"Yeah? Well, you haven't exactly been too nice lately yourself."

This wasn't starting off too well. "I wanted to talk to you..."

"You are. I haven't got all day. Like I said, what do you want?"

"I want to ask if you will contribute toward equipment for the baby, and then some child support after he's born."

"You must be fucking kidding me! You expect money from me?"

"No. Jacob. I don't expect anything from you." Now I was angry. "I am not asking you to support me in any way. I am asking you to support our child."

"Fuck you, Marnie! It's your child, just like your house and your car. Don't drag me into this." The phone went dead.

I sat still, phone in hand, glad that Sunshine didn't have to hear that conversation. In an odd way, pushing itself up through my anger was a sense of peace. That was that then. He didn't want to be involved with our son any more than he did with me. My heart ached for my unborn son who would never know the love of his father. I lifted my chin and straightened my shoulders. One good thing had come from this call. I knew where we stood, and I was surprisingly not sad over the loss of my relationship with Jake. I was okay. I could do this.

I considered my options; now that there was nobody else to consult, it would be so much easier. I contemplated my life in Alberta. It had been a wonderful safe haven to run to when I'd left my husband and was in search of life experiences. An exciting party place in my years, where I didn't feel judged, the place where I'd learned to drive a truck and gained my independence. But was it where I needed to be now? I thought of all the people that I knew. Most of them from nightclubs and bars, most of them childless or with support of family who would help out with babysitting duties. The only people I could rely on for help would be my friends Janet and Amanda. No, that wouldn't be fair. Janet herself was a single mom, and Amanda was too busy falling head over heels in love. Red Deer, Alberta had been my escape, but it wasn't my future. My 'network' was largely made up of freewheeling clubbers. If I cut myself off from them, I would be truly alone, a single parent in every respect. If I didn't, I'd probably be a terrible parent. I couldn't see us in this house, or in this town.

I mulled over options for a few weeks. Sunshine was becoming a reality. He needed a home, a family, and a 'proper' name. One night, I dreamed that I'd been chasing a small blond boy who was running and giggling. I called out to him, "Toby! Toby, wait for me." I was laughing too. It was one of those dreams that stayed with me long after I woke. Toby? Tobias? He would be Toby. No names that could be shortened. I hated my name being shortened to 'Marn,' and Toby couldn't be shortened. I started thinking about where we could live. If the decline in invitations and company since I'd given up drinking was anything to go by, Red Deer held little draw for me. I was free. Free to start again. I started looking at different areas. But the thought of being all alone, a stranger in a strange town while adjusting to single parenthood, was even less appealing. That narrowed things down a bit. The only places I really knew other than Red Deer were Willowdale, where I'd grown up, Pickering, where Will and I had lived, and nearby Markham, where we'd worked.

I was discussing these options with one of my few friends who hadn't dropped me the minute I gave up alcohol, when she said, "You know that, once Toby's born, you'll need Jacob's permission to move out of the province, right?"

"You can't be serious!" I was shocked. "He doesn't want anything to do with me, and he won't pay any child support. How does he get a say in where we live?"

"Marnie, he's still officially Toby's dad. Even if he doesn't pay anything, or even see him."

I gaped at her. My heartbeat was accelerating, and my cheeks burned with indignation. Was I forever going to be controlled by Jacob?

"Listen. I'm sorry, I'm just telling you what I know. Why don't you talk to a lawyer? I'm not a pro, I don't know all the ins and outs."

"I can't believe it. It's just so bloody unfair. He doesn't have to do anything he doesn't want to do, and I can't do anything without his permission? How does that even happen in this day and age?"

The next day, I called a lawyer I'd met socially, and she confirmed that even if Jacob wasn't paying child support, I would need his permission to leave the province with Toby. "Once he's born, that is..." She paused a moment, as if unsure whether or not to continue. Then, as if she'd made up her mind, she continued, "...but, until your child is born, you can relocate anywhere you like. While it's still inside of you, it is part of you. According to Canadian law, a fetus is not a legal person, and therefore, has no legal rights. This means that the biological father has no rights over your pregnancy unless you grant them to him. Once the child is born, it's a different story. You wouldn't need permission from the father to have an abortion, nor to move prior to the birth. I suggest that, once it's born, you approach the courts for financial support.

Canadian law stipulates that a child is entitled to the financial support of two parents, regardless of visitations."

A fetus. I couldn't think of Toby as a 'fetus.' He was the little blond boy that appeared in my dreams; there were less than three months to go until his arrival. Three short months. I needed to start making plans now; otherwise, we'd be stuck in Alberta and at Jacob's mercy forever. I'd have to sell my house. I could start there. But then what? Then I'd be pregnant and homeless. So much for freedom!

I did what most 'girls' would do. I phoned my mother. She wasn't impressed.

"You're about to have a baby, Marnie. I don't think now's the time to be selling your house and moving. Don't you think that you owe it to your child to make an effort to reconcile with its father?"

"No. I don't, Mom. I've already tried that. He's a deadbeat and will be more of a liability than a 'father.' If he's not drunk, or high, he's missing. Sometimes for days. What I need is get out of here before Toby's born; otherwise, we're going to be stuck here. I'm not asking your permission. I'm telling you my plan. But I'm going to need somewhere to stay while my house is being sold. I am asking you if I can come home. Can I stay with you and Dad for a few months?"

"You can't possibly drive all the way from Alberta in your state, Marnie."

"Mom, I'm pregnant, not an invalid. I can do it; I just want to know if I can stay with you?"

"Of course you can stay with us. But you're not driving on your own. I'll fly out and drive back with you."

I realized that tone of voice from my youth. She had made a decision and wasn't going to back down. No point in arguing. Actually, I didn't feel like arguing. Mom might not say "I love you," but her maternal instinct was expressed in practical ways. It would be a long trip, and a lot of time out of her busy schedule.

"Thanks, Mom."

"I still think you need to think this through properly. Call me when you've made up your mind."

"I don't have time, Mom, and my mind is made up."

"Right then. I'll book my ticket."

I put my phone down and paused for a moment to accept the decision I'd announced as 'made.' It was really happening. I looked around the house I'd lived in for so many years. I wasn't sure if I'd miss it or not. I'd spent so many miserable lonely nights here, and nearly ended my child's and my life here. There had been good times too, though. I thought of Jake. We'd had a lot of fun together in the beginning. He was like a child. Charming and fun when things were going his way and sulks and tantrums when they weren't. He wasn't bad, really, just irresponsible. I'd received heaps of traffic fines in the mail after my return from Mexico, the photos all taken in the early hours of the morning. He hadn't volunteered to pay them. That's what I was for. I wondered at our relationship. Did he ever actually love me? And, why did I think I could compete with Sarah? She was way younger than Jake, and I was way older. The age gap between her and me couldn't be much less than the one between my mother and me. Not that I'd planned to compete with Sarah. She was part of Jacob's past when we got together. If I'd realized that he wasn't completely over her, I'm not sure that I'd have gotten involved with him.

I looked down at my now bulging belly and gave it a rub. "Sunshine... Toby, your mom's an idiot. You can't get more 'involved' than this right? Not long now, I can't wait to see you. To hold you." On a whim, I picked up my phone again, and dialed Jake's number. I couldn't go without saying goodbye.

"Hi, Jake. I just wanted to let you know that I'm thinking of moving to Toronto." Why did I say 'thinking?' I'd just told my mom I was going. For sure.

"You wouldn't fucking dare." Like a bucket of cold water on a small flame, my sentimentality turned to steam. I could almost see it rising off me and disappearing into the ether.

"Jacob. You really don't know me. I would definitely dare. I'm going. This is just a courtesy call to let you know."

"Fuck your 'courtesy,' Marnie. You can't move to another province with my child. I won't allow it. I know you better than you know yourself. You haven't got the balls."

No. I didn't have balls. Not physically. But, challenge accepted. It was time to put the wheels into motion for me and my child.

Chapter 3:

The Travel Seed Takes Root

My son, Toby McBain, was born on the 19th of September, 2008. Thirteen days earlier than anticipated. On that day, my life changed irrevocably. I was committed for life, needed by an innocent, defenseless, beautiful baby. I was also no longer pregnant and gave myself permission to drink alcohol again. The two were not compatible, but I chose to believe that they could be balanced, and that the daily responsibility of motherhood meant that I was entitled to an escape from time to time. My parents did not agree. Despite their condemnation of my pregnancy, they loved their grandson.

The end result was that I graduated from 'disappointing-child' to 'disappointing-parent.' When would I ever settle down and take life seriously? It didn't help that for the first two months of Toby's life, we were living in my parents' 840-square-foot cottage with them while I waited for the sale of my house in Alberta, and the purchase of my new home in Ontario, to go through. Credit to my parents, though, they coped well with this invasion of their space, and my mom was generous with her advice. She taught me how to bathe Toby in the kitchen sink and create a sitz bath out of a bucket (as they only had a shower). She was always there to give me practical tips on parenting. My dad was smitten by his first-born grandchild.

Twenty-seven days after Toby's birth, my ever-obliging brother hit his first proud milestone, becoming a father to Travis, and then two years later, to Carter. Both boys. In the eyes of society, these grandsons were an achievement worthy of celebration. After all, James and Karen had been living together for some years. The shame that sullied Toby's birth did not apply.

On the three-day road trip from Alberta, during my pregnancy, my mother had made her feelings clear on the subject of my pending single parenthood. My father stood by my mother. Ironically, Jacob's word, 'dare' came up a lot in these conversations. "Marnie, how dare you deprive your child of his father!" I heard this often, until one day I snapped and screamed back, "What the hell is your problem? How can you even think that Toby would be better off with an abusive, drunk, drug addict in his life? Do you really want us tied into a relationship like that, just to legitimise my pregnancy? I don't care what your friends think!" That closed the subject, but it remained a fundamental problem expressed in actions and silent disapproval rather than words.

Toby and I moved into our new home when he was two months old. It was both exciting and scary at the same time. I was in love with my house. Not much to look at from the outside, but perfectly me on the inside. My parents both recognized the importance of having extra income rental, and my dad worked like a trojan with a contractor to convert the basement to a second apartment. This was not the first time he'd helped me to renovate a house for additional income. It relieved my financial pressures enormously, and I'll forever be grateful to him for all his practical help over the years. My savings were dwindling, and I didn't like the feeling. I may not be the most conservative person; I couldn't bear the thought of being tied to a gray job, living a gray life, but I was and still am frugal. While I wanted the freedom to explore and live life on my own terms (usually flying by the seat of my pants), I still wanted to have a little security blanket to tide me over in uncertain times.

Living with tenants in the basement came with its own challenges. If I wasn't stressing about their noise waking Toby, I was stressing about Toby's cries disturbing them. It felt as though I was always trying to balance things to keep everyone around me happy. They were nice people and didn't complain unnecessarily. The stress was more self-inflicted than a result of them being intolerant. All in all, though, the income was welcome, and it was a fair trade.

I was truly a single parent now. In every sense of the word. There was no such thing as 'time out.' I was hungry for intellectual stimulation. I was also desperate for sleep. There is nothing as precious as watching your child sleep, seeing the rise and fall of his little chest, his vulnerability and fragility when he is completely at ease. I sadly didn't see much of that in the first 14 months of Toby's life. He seemed to never sleep, and when he did, I had to quickly try and get some shut-eye too. It would not be an exaggeration to say that the maximum hours of consecutive sleep I got during that period was four hours. I was exhausted mentally and physically.

I smarted every time my parents arranged to babysit for James and Karen so they could have a 'well earned' date night. I begged for time out to be by myself, go shopping without Toby in tow. On occasion, my parents would help out for an hour or two, but in general, the response was, "Marnie, you got yourself into this situation, you should have thought it through before getting pregnant. You need to deal with the consequences of your actions." It felt almost as though, as much as they loved Toby, my parents thought I had not yet paid enough penance for my unplanned pregnancy. The guilt I felt at burdening my parents with my selfishness was overwhelming.

So was my exhaustion. I eventually called my mother one day and said simply, "I can't do this anymore. Please, can you take Toby for the weekend? I am desperate. I need to sleep. If you can't help me, then I'm going to call the Children's Aid Society and report myself. I'm losing my mind and it's not good for Toby."

"Okay, Marnie. No need for the dramatics. We'll take him. But you need to drop him off and pick him up."

The relief was intense. I dropped him off at 4 p.m. on Friday, and headed straight home. Sleep was more important than intellectual stimulation. I wouldn't have been able to hold a sensible conversation anyway. This would be the first time I'd be away from Toby for more than a couple of hours. Sleep deprivation dulled the remorse that I felt at leaving my baby. This was as much for him as it was for me. Surely in two days, I'd make up enough sleep to be a better mom on his return. I'd be more patient when he didn't sleep, and less depressed.

I thanked my parents profusely, and kissed Toby goodbye, feeling quite tearful. "I'll be back on Sunday to get you, my little man." The drive home was difficult. It was almost as though my body, knowing that it was going to be allowed to rest, had given up trying to stay awake. I wasn't aware of my surroundings, and drove by rote. Mind numb.

Safely home, by sheer luck rather than skill, I selected Pink Floyd's "Comfortably Numb" on my playlist and crawled into bed. My body became heavy, and the words seemed to float around me. The singer was calling out to me, asking if I could hear him, if I was home, offering to ease my pain and get me on my feet again. I wished he could.

Now I was floating. Floating light as a feather, buoyed by the haunting music and distorted words. Drifting into oblivion.

I woke to the insistent tune of my mobile. It took me a moment to realize that I was at home, in my bed. I looked at the time. It was twelve o' clock. By the light flooding in, it was obviously midday, not midnight. I fumbled for the phone. "Mom?"

"Marnie, I just wanted to check with you what time you're fetching Toby?"

"Is it Sunday already?" It didn't feel as though I'd been asleep long at all. It couldn't be Sunday. Surely?

"No. It's Saturday. Dad and I have dinner plans for tonight. Do you think you could be here in the next hour or two?"

"Okay, Mom. I'm coming." I cut the call and burst into tears. My sleep had been snatched from me. I didn't know whether the mistake was mine or my mother's; I didn't even care. I didn't have the energy to care. I had to conserve it because I was back on duty with my batteries only half charged.

It was two months before I dared ask again. Toby had finally been weaned, and we were going to Mexico with my parents. I asked if I could have two days to myself, and they agreed. I dropped them and Toby off at an all-inclusive resort, then headed to the neighboring town where I'd booked an Airbnb for myself. I went out to dinner, had an early night, and explored the next day. It felt incredibly free to not have to consult with anyone, or take anyone else into consideration. I could walk on the beach if I wanted to. I could eat and sleep when I wanted to. On the second night, I fell into bed at 7 p.m. and woke the next afternoon at 3 p.m. I'd missed my checkout time! I scrambled to get my things together and go and join my parents.

At the resort, after dinner, my parents were heading to bed, and I was feeling like a new person. "Will you take Toby for tonight?" I asked. "I slept all day and I'd like to stay up and listen to the band for a bit."

I knew I was pushing it. But it had been a relaxed evening, and I was feeling refreshed, so I just put it out there. To my surprise, my mom agreed.

"Don't be up too late."

"I won't," I promised.

The next day. when we met for breakfast. my mother looked at me sceptically. "Have a late night last night?"

I shook my head. It hadn't been late by my standards. I'd been in bed before midnight.

"You were drinking." It was a statement, not a question.

"Yes. But not too much." I saw the disappointment tightening her face and pulling down the corners of her mouth.

"You're a mother, Marnie."

"I know, Mom. But so's Karen. How come you never talk to her like this?"

"This isn't about Karen. This is about you."

It always came back to me. I actually didn't drink as much as my brother and his partner. I thought that maybe that was half the problem. I wasn't drinking fit, so got drunk more quickly and took longer to recover. The end result, though, was that from then on, every time I tried to get my folks to babysit, I was hard pressed to convince them that it wasn't because I wanted to get blind drunk. That was never my intention when going out; I just wanted to feel free for a while, but it was sadly quite often the outcome. I only discovered much later in life, that much of this could actually be attributed to my vegetarian diet. It seems that a big steak goes a long way toward increasing your alcohol tolerance. I don't know how scientifically true that is, but it's my story and I'm sticking to it.

Funnily enough, in my early days of breastfeeding Toby, I'd had cravings for protein and had broken my 'diet' to wolf down a steak. I felt guilty, but it was delicious. Thereafter, I became a flexitarian, eating whatever my body demanded of me. I figured this was because my blood type was B, meaning I needed little protein in my diet, but Toby was type O, and it was his needs that I needed to fulfil.

One good thing that came of the amount of one-on-one time spent with Toby was the fact that I got to know him so well that, within a few weeks, we'd been connected to the extent that I could sense when he needed to poop or pee. I knew his routines, and realized his little movements and wriggles. I found a book called *Diaper Free* and immediately put the suggestions into practice. By the time Toby was 12 weeks old, he'd pooped in a diaper for the last time. I was able to get him over a toilet or sink every time. I only used diapers on him at night (in somewhat misguided optimistic anticipation of a good night's sleep). They were rarely wet in the mornings.

I hadn't only stayed home in Toby's first two years. I'd made two forays into the world of employment in that period. Both were abysmal disasters that lasted only a few months each. The first because the cost of child care for Toby was almost equal to my salary. It didn't take me long to realize that all I was doing was cheating my son out of time with his mother, for no benefit. The second, because my boss was a hopeless flirt; well, more than that. At first, I thought I could deal with it, but when he started getting touchy-feely, I didn't know how to cope anymore. I felt guilt; the 'slut' label that always lurked in the recesses of my mind became a looping thought. It permeated my dreams. I stressed about it. I spent hours agonizing over my words and actions, trying to identify behavior that might have encouraged his interest. I modified my behavior on a daily basis, changing from friendly and helpful to borderline rude. Nothing helped. I couldn't report the issue for fear of bringing more shame on my family, and turning the 'slut' spotlight back on me. I had also become quite concerned about the way that he did business. Best business practices were fairy tales in his mind. The easiest solution was to resign.

On the very last day of the year in 2009, I had a blind date. I'd met Kevin on the Internet, just about the only place for housebound-single-moms to meet anyone. Despite having chatted online for some time, I was incredibly nervous. I hadn't dated for a while and, of course, not having any friends in common, I couldn't get the low down on him. So, when he called, I was a bit hesitant.

"Marnie, it's time we met in person. Why don't we celebrate the new year together?"

"Um. Yeah, sure, that sounds nice. But…I don't really know how to go about this… I think maybe lunch?" It would be easier to find a babysitter at lunchtime than at night, and if he was a total creep, somehow meeting a creep in the daytime seemed less frightening than at night.

"Okay." He didn't seem concerned about me making it a daytime function. "I'll come and pick you up."

"Uh. No, it's okay. I've got a car. Tell me where you want to meet and I'll see you there." I wasn't giving him my address. I'd read enough horror stories.

He laughed. "Okay, I haven't decided where yet, but I'll send you the details, okay?"

"Okay." My hand was shaking slightly. "Um…I mean, thanks. Thanks, I'm looking forward to it." I'd nearly forgotten my manners.

Early in the morning of the 31st of December, I was dozily breastfeeding Toby when I suddenly remembered. Today was the day. I looked at the top of his silky golden head. "Mommy's got a date today, my little man," I whispered. He suckled on, oblivious to my nerves.

I spent ages going through my wardrobe, trying to select the right outfit, and discussing each with Toby, while he just regarded me steadily with his blue eyes. "What about this?" I said, holding up the clothes hanger. Toby didn't react. "Okay, maybe you're right. Too sexy. He might be a lech. And this?" I wiggled the hanger and he giggled. I laughed too. "Yeah, a bit too prim. I'll look like a school teacher. Damn, Toby, this is hard." I took outfit number five from the wardrobe and held it against me. Toby lunged forward and made a grab at the fabric. I scooped him up in my free arm and planted a kiss on his head. "Yeah! That's it then, my sunshine. You're the best fashion adviser." We twirled around the room for a moment, me, my boy, and the chosen outfit.

Eventually, dressed, looking half-decent and warm enough to face the freezing outdoors, I was ready to go. I held Toby tight as I rushed out the door to take him to a friend. Oops! Not so fast. My shoes slipped on the icy path. I righted myself and narrowly missed landing butt down in the snow. That would have hurt without hands free to break the fall. As I buckled Toby into his carseat, I glimpsed the snow piled up on the trunk. No time to clear it off; it would have to blow off as I drove. I ran around to the driver's side, leapt in, closed the car door quickly, and fumbled with the keys. I wasn't sure whether it was the cold or nerves, probably a bit of both. I really felt like a schoolgirl on her first date!

Finally, the key turned in the ignition. The car lurched forward and crunched into the closed garage door as my foot slipped off the clutch. Damn! I'd forgotten that I'd left it in gear last night to avoid using the emergency brake, which tended to freeze in winter. I jammed my foot onto the clutch just in time to prevent the car from stalling, put it into neutral, and released the clutch. The metal of the door creaked as it twisted and crumpled, scraping the paint from the new car. I heard the headlights shatter and tinkle as they landed on the concrete floor, then the sound of the tires scrunching over the broken glass. The entire hood of the car was now inside the closed garage—right up to the windshield. I felt paralyzed inside, and was kind of surprised that my body still functioned. Toby was quiet. I looked at him, fearing that he might have been hurt. But no. He was just sitting there, looking at me wide-eyed as if waiting for my response before deciding how to react.

I leapt out of the car, and called Kevin to say that I'd be late. He sounded skeptical. I later learned that he'd thought I had cold feet.

I eventually made it to the bar, about an hour late, my car clunking its way into the parking lot. I was sick with apprehension, not just about the date, but at the huge costs I'd just incurred by wrecking my car and my garage door.

I recognized Kevin immediately. At 6-foot-tall, with his signature shoulder-length, prematurely gray hair, he was easy to pick out from the crowd. He had a wide smile, which he used often and to great effect. Conversation flowed easily, we shared a dry, slightly quirky sense of humor, and both saw the funny side of life in little things. He was a snarky Star Trek fan, my kind of guy. When he ordered his second beer, the waitress asked him if he'd like lime with his beer. "No, thanks, no lime." About 15 minutes later, another waitress approached him and asked him again if he'd like lime with his beer. He shook his head, and responded again, "No, thanks. No lime."

I had a couple of drinks too, and when it came time to head home, we had swapped phone numbers and were talking about a second date.

So, began a special friendship. We really enjoyed each other's company, but decided that romance was not in the cards. We talked often, hung out together, and even went on camping trips with the kids; he had three girls. It was on one of these camping trips that he told me that the bar we'd had our first date at was his regular haunt, and that the waitresses were primed to ask him if he'd like lime with his beer. If he said 'yes,' that was their signal to fake an emergency call, giving him an excuse to escape a tedious date.

I was a bit concerned about his drinking. I know, I probably sound like my mother, but he always seemed to have one or two too many. I put this down to the fact that I only saw him socially when he was relaxed. He eventually moved away to Ottawa, and I missed his company. He'd become a special friend who was always there for me. He still is to this day. But I didn't see much of him because of the distance. One day, I arranged a surprise visit, with the help of his daughters' mother, and took his daughters up to Ottawa to see him. We kept our secret well, and the look of utter amazement and joy on his face when he answered the door was a reward in itself.

We stayed up late that night, chatting and drinking, long after the kids had been put to bed. Once or twice, I made half-hearted attempts at ending the evening, but we were both having so much fun and enjoying catching up, that we ended up sharing deep thoughts while staring deep into the bottle. We must have seriously bonded over those deep thoughts, because I woke up in his bed the next morning! I lay still in the bed, not daring to move for fear of waking Kevin. My heart and head were pounding. What the hell had we done? I peeked under the sheet. No clothes. It was perfectly clear what had happened. I tried to remember the prelude to all this, but my memory faded at a point when we'd still been sitting in the living room, arms around each other and my head resting on his shoulder. Oh God!

I slid gingerly out of the bed and retrieved my clothes from the floor before fleeing to the bathroom to shower and dress. What the hell had we been thinking? I went to the kitchen and grabbed an energy drink before getting the kids dressed and ready for the day. I flushed as I picked up their pyjamas and underwear. I wondered if they'd be that happy if they knew that last night, while they were sleeping, I had been naked in bed with their father.

I was busy brushing hair for the youngest when he wandered into the room. "Hello, beautiful," he said with a smile. I flushed a hot red, and his smile broadened. Clearly, one of us remembered the night before.

Thus began a relationship that probably should never have been, but one that I don't regret. We had been right when we'd first decided that we were better suited to the friend zone than a romantic relationship. One of the things I really loved about him was his unconditional acceptance of me. I never had to pretend around him. He accepted me with all my flaws. Except when he was roaring drunk. And unfortunately, the more time I spent with him, the more I became aware of how often this happened. He had no 'off' switch. I would often be happy to join in, my off switch being fairly flexible and slightly faulty itself. It would never have occurred to me to have a beer at seven o'clock in the morning. Even I, with my dodgy moral compass, was shocked by that.

One night, well, early morning to be honest, about 02h00, Kevin and I were at my home, we'd both had a few drinks, and we were delving into our deepest fears and hopes—in vino veritas and all that. Okay, I was doing the delving into mine, and Kevin was just agreeing and being super supportive.

"I totally get it, Marnie. You have to live your life."

"Yeah. Why do I have to keep living by everyone else's rules? I don't want to be a suburban mom. I don't want to pretend that I'm not interested in wicca, or shut up about my premonitions. It's not true to me. How can I be a mother if I'm always being a fraud? Why isn't being me good enough?"

"Being you is good enough. It's just hard for your family 'cause they don't understand. They think their way is the only way."

"Well, I can't keep going like this. But I can't afford not to. Oh, man. Life is so hard. And there's Toby. I have to think about him too. I'm not my own person anymore. I'm Toby's person... How does that happen to women? You go from being someone's daughter to someone's wife to someone's mother. When do I get to be me—just me?"

"Hey, Toby loves you. He doesn't care what your interests are or how you dress. He's too young; he just sees his mom and he accepts you as you are. You can be his mother and yourself at the same time."

"Yeah, but I can't do things because of Toby—"

"Like what? What would you be doing if you had never gotten pregnant?"

"I'd be traveling. For sure. I want to see the world; I want to find people like me. I'd probably be living in a hippie commune in Mexico."

"Yeah, but it's not Toby's fault you're not doing that. You wouldn't be able to afford it."

"No. I could. I could rent out my house and buy a truck and RV. I could work on the road. I could."

"Then what's stopping you? And don't say Toby. If you can live in a trailer, so could Toby. In fact, if there was ever a perfect time to do it, it would be now. Before he starts school."

I looked at him in wonder. Here was this man, telling me that I was the only thing standing between myself and the 'real life' I'd always yearned for. He was right! I was almost 40 years old, and I had to stop being a people pleaser. I had to stop making excuses and blaming others for my unhappiness. It was my time to live.

I felt a sudden urgency. I needed to get things rolling now. Before I got scared or talked out of it. Before I could sober up too much. Right now, I could see with great clarity that the world had just opened up in front of me. I had to seize the day! Strike while the iron was hot! Get things sorted before I lost sight of this incredible vision.

I grabbed my computer and started searching Google. I needed to find tenants for my house. I needed to buy a truck and trailer. Quickly, before this extraordinary lucidity evaporated. I got onto Kijiji, Canada's answer to Craigslist, where you can "buy, sell or trade almost anything! New and used items, cars, real estate, jobs…" Perfect.

I put my home up for rent, and my car for sale (thank goodness it was fixed after its garage door incident). After a short debate on which was better, an RV or a trailer, I put in an offer on a combination deal for a truck and a fifth-wheel trailer. There would be less that could go wrong with a trailer, I could park it then explore with the truck, and I wasn't scared of towing. Hell, I'd done enough of that in Alberta after I got my license. I laughed and told Kevin how shocked my family had been.

"Here I was, so proud of myself for learning to drive a truck, and when I told my brother, all he could say was 'Mom's going to lose her shit!'" I giggled. "Funny that, because my first truck driving job after I qualified was spreading manure."

He laughed. "Typical Marnie, and you haven't stopped since." I cuffed him playfully on the back of his head. He mock-winced. "What'd your mom say?"

I mimicked my mom. "Oh my God, Marnie! What am I going to tell my friends? I can't tell them my daughter is a truck driver!"

We both howled with laughter. I was on a roll.

"And... And... The oil companies were all advertising for truck drivers and paying for them to qualify! I thought I had such a great plan. Only I discovered they were only paying for learners with penises. I had the wrong equipment—so I had to pay."

"Bloody chauvinists!" Kevin laughed. "I'm glad you haven't got a penis."

"At my first lesson, I asked the instructor to show me the inside of a truck, 'cause I'd never seen one. He nearly choked!"

We laughed. We high-fived, and we poured another drink to toast my new life on the road—living by my rules.

The next morning, I discovered that Kijiji really did live up to its claims. I already had a prospective tenant for my home, and my offer on the truck and trailer had been accepted. Now to break the news to the family. I already knew that the decision to take off and travel with my two-year-old wasn't going to go down well. I needed to be prepared for their arguments. I sat down and wrote out a list of pros and cons, from their perspective and from mine. On 'my' list, the pros far outnumbered the cons. In fact, there was only one con: finances. On 'their' list, the pros still outweighed the cons, but there was more than one con. My parents would definitely view Toby's and my time away from them as a con. They were bound to bring up my brother's family too. Of course, life revolved around James and his family. How often does that happen? That the child living closer to the parents, and more involved in their daily lives, is open to criticism, while the one that only shows up for high days and holidays is beyond reproach?

I could justify this adventure to my parents and defend my right to live my life the way I please and bring Toby up successfully on the road. But could I justify the cost? I needed to do the sums and work out what the costs would actually be. After drawing up a budget, it was apparent that it could be done—but it couldn't be done in style. That was okay. Style had never really been my thing anyway. I didn't really know where I wanted to go, and I didn't want to tie myself down to an unrealistic itinerary, so budgeting was complicated. I knew I needed to go beyond Canada. I wanted to head for America and sunny weather. I would take Toby to the ocean. I researched trailer parks, exciting places, and cheap places. I discovered a wonderful innovation. While campsites with facilities on Bureau of Land Management grounds attracted a fee, dispersed camping on BLM land, near but not in the established campsites, for up to days was free. That made a world of difference to my budget. It took it from almost impossible to doable if we ate cheaply.

I could eat cheaply. And Toby, though he was no longer breastfeeding, was not a fussy eater. Like most toddlers, his favourite foods were simple. Bread, pasta, and fruit ranking higher than anything else. I was happy with the same. Having been a vegetarian for many years, I was quite capable of having cheap, meat-free meals.

The announcement went down as anticipated. My parents were trying their best to put on a show of support, but I knew in my heart that they were not happy. This was confirmed when I overheard them saying to Toby, "You should tell your mommy that you want to have a house to live in." I said nothing when I entered the room. But the quick glance between my parents made it clear that they suspected they'd been overheard. I chose not to debate what I saw as underhanded tactics in front of Toby. Maybe. Maybe, I just thought that if I pretended not to have heard, I wouldn't have to acknowledge or deal with their opposition to my travel plans. We could both continue to pretend that we were on the same page. I liked the role of supportive parents that they'd adopted, and I wasn't going to do anything to shake that.

In anticipation of our departure, my parents started trying to spend as much time with Toby and I as they could. I welcomed their closer involvement, but nothing was going to change my mind. Toby and I were going to hit the road. I needed space to be me. I needed to bond with Toby and bring him up my way. He was my son all right. I listened with frustration one day when my father, after I'd declined to have Toby spend time with them because we had plans, resorted to dirty tactics, saying, "Toby, Grandpa will buy you an ice cream if you stay with us."

Toby looked from my father to me, then said, "I have to go with Mom." My heart expanded with love and pride. Then he looked up at me again, "Will you buy me an ice cream now, Mom?" My son and future travel companion was turning out to be a wily negotiator.

Chapter 4:

On the Road with Toby

On the 2nd of November, 2010, I woke early, partly because I'd slept the night on the floor, with my house all packed up and rented out, and partly from excitement. The big day had arrived, and my boy and I were going to be hitting the road!

Our departure was a month later than originally planned because a number of things went wrong. The truck I'd bought turned out to be too small to pull the trailer, I broke my ankle, Kevin and I broke up after he got cited for driving under the influence of alcohol and blamed me, and my new tenant had pulled out of the contract.

After purchasing the truck and trailer online, I'd left Toby with my parents for four days while I flew to Alberta to pick them up. Immediately after hitting the road, on what should have been a three-day drive back home, I discovered that there was no way that this truck could manage the 27-foot trailer. Even with the trailer empty, the truck struggled. It would be impossible once loaded with water and provisions.

So instead of heading home, I'd stopped in Medicine Hat and prevailed on my cousins, Johnny and Dave, to accommodate me while I tried to find a bigger truck. This meant spending an additional $500 that wasn't budgeted for, losing an additional four days, and leaving a very active two-year-old with my parents for longer than planned. I was amazed by how much I missed Toby. The first day or two might have felt like a fun adventure, being free to be selfish, but by day three, I was yearning for a cuddle and kept finding myself phrasing commentary on things I was seeing, but unable to deliver it because he was not there. A part of me was missing. Finally, as I was losing hope, and my cousins were no doubt losing patience, I found a truck, two and a half hours' drive from their home. What a great truck! A 1996, GMC Dually Diesel, five-speed transmission.

I bought it on the spot. Then immediately started to stress again. I now owned 2 trucks and my budget for the trip was just about nonexistent. I often think that the universe directs me, though, and this occasion was no different. As I was collecting my new truck, a buyer called wanting to look at the little truck. He and I arrived in Medicine Hat within minutes of each other, and the deal was done. Even more serendipitous, he didn't need the 5th wheel hitch, so I had it moved to the GMC and we both went our merry ways. I left for home the same day, and my new truck drove like there was no trailer attached. It just ate up the kilometers, and I covered the 4000 kilometers to my boy in just two days.

When my tenant pulled out, I thought I'd really messed up and the whole trip was going to be scuppered. I agonised, worrying about having bought the truck and trailer, and now being stuck with no tenant. I started to think that this trip wasn't destined to happen. I decided to once again put it out there for the universe to decide. I listed the truck and trailer for sale, and my house to rent, on Kijiji and waited to see which would go first. If the truck and trailer sold, I was going to cut my losses. If I got a tenant, that would be my sign that our journey was meant to be.

By the next day, I had another prospective tenant and still owned the truck and trailer.

I didn't plan an itinerary. All I knew was that we were heading to the USA and in the direction of the Gulf coast. I pre-planned one or two stops to see friends along the way, but very little else. Our first day on the road was a short one. I drove from Peterborough to Niagara Falls; it took about five hours, an hour longer than planned.

I had visited the falls before, but it was going to be Toby's first experience there, and I found myself buoyed with excitement. Having arrived bright and early, we had time to explore the area. Toby was every bit as impressed as I'd hoped. The roar of the water was audible even from the carpark, and grew louder and louder as we approached the mass of plunging water. My little man was most amused by the 'rain' that wet us every time the mist from the thundering falls drifted across on the breeze; equally enchanting was the multi-colored rainbow that shimmered in front of the tumbling sheets of water. Toby was keen to touch the rainbow, and I had a hard time trying to explain why this wasn't possible. His enquiring mind and enthusiasm were contagious.

We went to bed early and spent a very comfortable night in the driveway of my parents' friends. So far, so good.

The following morning, we headed for the US border via the Queenston-Lewiston bridge. As we pulled up at the border post, Toby pointed. "Look, Mommy! Soldiers." I followed the direction of his chubby little finger and saw a convoy of seven Dodge RAM trucks, camouflaged in splodges of green and brown, each sporting a gun rack bristling with rifles.

"Hmm…I don't think they're soldiers, Toby. They look like hunters."

"What's a hunter?"

"Someone who shoots animals."

He looked shocked, and scared. "Why do they shoot animals, Mommy?"

"Mostly to eat, I guess. But for fun too."

"Do they shoot them dead?"

"Yes."

"That's not fun. That's mean!"

"I agree."

"But why then?"

I sighed. "I don't really understand either, little man, but not everybody does things that we like. People are different."

"Did you ever shoot an animal?"

"No! I never would. I don't even like guns."

"Me neither."

With that, we entered the border patrol office, listening with half an ear to the famous southern drawl coming from the vociferous group of men. At the front of the queue, the border official asked, "How long will you be staying in the US?"

"Six months," I responded, resisting the childish urge to cross my fingers behind my back. Actually, I had no idea. If I found a nice hippie commune to join, I could definitely see us staying on. Maybe forever. There was no real reason for me to return to Canada, and the adventure was just beginning.

He weighed me up with a glance. "What about work?"

"I'm on leave of absence."

He leaned his head out of the window and looked at Toby. "Who is this lady?"

Toby giggled. "She's Mommy." The higher pitch of his voice on the word 'mommy' indicated the unsaid word 'silly.' Honestly! Imagine someone not knowing Mommy?

The official's face softened a bit. "And where are you going with Mommy?"

"Ocean! To the ocean."

With that, the paperwork was completed, my presence legitimised by a two-year-old, and we were headed oceanward.

It was hard to imagine spending time on the beach or swimming in the ocean. It was freezing cold, and we were bundled up in our winter woollies as we traveled through New York state, heading for Pennsylvania where my ex-colleague from the Alberta oil fields, Sharlene, awaited us. I had discovered that something was amiss with the trailer. The furnace in the fifth-wheeler only worked sporadically for one cycle of about an hour at a time, in between which I needed to head outside and give it a thwack with a hammer to get it going again; not ideal at night in the freezing cold. This was yet another expense I hadn't bargained on. Goodness alone knows how much the furnace would cost to fix. Most of my very tight budget was allocated to fuel.

That was a serious dilemma. In order to stay in certain parks, your trailer had to match certain criteria (including the age of your trailer), and in order to camp for free on BLM lands, you needed to be completely self-sufficient. There would be no power to heat the trailer.

My tight financial situation pricked at my conscience as I drove. I started to question my motives for this journey, given that it wasn't something I could easily afford. Was I crazy, wanting to bring my son up my way, without interference from society and extended family? My parents might be inclined to think that I was being over-controlling and determined to buck the system.

Was I selfish because I didn't want to work? I didn't think so. What little I brought in from work had almost all gone to childcare. So, to me, it made sense to not work. Not that my brother would ever see it that way. He had a special disdain for single mothers who were on the dole, or off large child support payments from guilty fathers. I was neither on the dole, nor did I receive any child support from Jacob. Despite having petitioned the courts for it.

Or had I made this decision from a place of love? There was no doubt in my mind that I loved my son and I wanted him to be brought up by me, not by a childminder. To be honest, I was also dodging the whole global village scenario too. I didn't love the way society made me feel, and wanted to bring Toby up shielded from all that disapproval. I wanted Toby to be free. I did. I also wanted me to be free. Little did I realize at that stage how much more responsibility I was taking on by shunning the shackles of society, and how ill-equipped I was to deal with it.

There is very little that society does to prepare new parents for parenthood—whether single or not. I heard someone say once that this is deliberate. Nobody wants young people (not that I was young in the strict sense of the word) to know just how tough it really is, because that might result in major population reduction. So, everybody struggles along, doing their best and not breaking the code of silence. At school, you can learn how to make babies—but are given very little information on how to look after them, or how they make you feel. Never mind the effect of the huge hormonal change on a new mother.

I thought about my early days of pregnancy when I'd still been trying to make things work with Jacob. Jake wouldn't give up drinking, or even cut back in solidarity with me. It was my pregnancy. He wouldn't have been able to breastfeed either, and I couldn't imagine him offering to 'help' with the housework, diapers, or baby baths. I'd have ended up looking after both Jake and Toby. I wondered how young couples managed life. Are there really men out there, who when their wives have given birth, think, "Yahoo! I'm getting my sex life back!" I couldn't even begin to think of trying to fit a romp in the hay into the pitiful hours of sleep time I'd got in Toby's first 14 months of life. Thank goodness that was one less demand on my time. How the hell do couples cope?

I peeked over my shoulder at Toby, who had dozed off in his carseat, a crayon clutched in his chubby little fist. He made my heart smile. So sweet. So innocent. He hadn't yet learned of the callousness of the world. I wanted to shield him from it, but I knew that he'd be better off if I could just teach him to deal with it without it getting inside his armor.

"I'd choose to have you again," I murmured. "You're worth so much more than sleep." He is my miracle.

Pulling up at Sharlene's, I was really excited to catch up with her. It would be the first time she and Toby would be meeting. She had been a wonderful friend in the old days. One of those incredible women that could do just about anything. She'd been my supervisor in the oil fields, and had later been transferred to a management position in the USA. She was a ground breaker, as far as senior positions for women in that particular company went.

Her driveway was, however, not built with a truck and trailer in mind, so after an aborted attempt at parking the trailer in her drive, I had to settle for parking on the side of the road in front of her house.

After a fun afternoon watching Toby and Sharlene bonding as they played in the leaves, we had a delicious dinner that I didn't have to cook. Then I plugged the trailer into Sharlene's electricity and put Toby to bed. When he finally fell asleep, I tiptoed out of the trailer, made my way across the lawn, and rapped on the front door to meet Sharlene for a drink and the long awaited catch up. The knocking set off a cacophony of vicious barks inside. It took Sharlene a few minutes to quiet her two over-enthusiastic pit bulls before she opened up. As I stepped in the door, I offered my hand to the front dog; he sniffed it and relaxed. The dogs knew me; I'd looked after them for Sharlene before.

As I turned to remove my jacket, my wrist was seized in a vise-like grip and I spun around, eyes watering from pain to see the pit bull tugging angrily at my arm. Sharlene lunged forward shouting, "No!" and grabbed at her dog. It took a big effort for her to get the dog to release its grip and then drag it to the basement. Once it was locked inside, whining like it was the injured party, she returned to inspect the damage.

"Oh shit, sorry, Marnie!" she apologized, inspecting my arm. Fortunately, my neoprene jacket had protected the skin, but the bruising to my wrist would be a reminder of that sudden loss of control. "I'm starting to think that dog is mental. He just seems to lose it every now and then."

About 18 months later, the same dog would attack Sharlene in her bed, and have to be put down.

I only stayed for one drink, and sat near the window, keeping an eye on the trailer with my sleeping toddler, but it was great to catch up on each other's news. Ours was one of those friendships that you can just pick up where you left off years later. It felt as if we'd only been apart for a weekend.

I snuggled into bed with Toby later that evening; my wrist throbbed, but I was happy. I'd had a good day, and now that we were plugged in to power, the trailer was snug inside. Tomorrow, I would find out how much the furnace was going to cost to fix. I didn't want to think about this unplanned expense. Tomorrow was another day.

I fell into a dreamless sleep, only to be woken by a thud. I lay still and heard distant voices and the sound of a stone hitting the trailer. Then another. I reached for my mobile to call Sharlene. Toby slept on. Another one. Then another. I switched on a light inside, and heard the sound of running feet thudding off into the distance. Switching the light off, I opened the curtains a crack and peered out into the darkness. A streetlight cast an eerie yellow light on the sidewalk. Everything was still. Whoever they were had gone; it was the middle of the night, no point in disturbing Sharlene. But I kept my mobile close by and lay awake for hours waiting for sleep to return.

Early in the morning, I stepped outside to inspect the damage. Ugh! It wasn't stones the trailer had been pelted with. It was eggs. Bits of eggshell were frozen against the sides of the trailer. I suspected that my Alberta plates had upset some of the locals, thinking I was after a job. Work was tight, and I didn't blame them for their feelings. I did blame them for the mess they'd made of my trailer, though. I didn't have time to deal with that now. I had more pressing problems, and time was ticking.

It was bloody cold in the trailer without the furnace, and rushing outside, hammer in hand, every hour was also not conducive to sleep or happiness. It was so cold. The kind of cold that no amount of clothing can block out. It seeped into our bones and intensified the ache in my wrist. I was worried about what it would cost to fix the furnace, and I didn't want to be fleeced again. I decided the furnace would have to wait until we reached Alabama, where friends of my parents, who were seasoned motorhome travelers, lived. They had contacts who would make sure that I got a fair deal on the repair.

I was tired, cold, sore, and out of sorts. Poor Toby. Actually, Toby was oblivious to all but the cold, and he was also on his best behavior. He played with his toys, colored in and stuck little stickers everywhere, including on himself. He seemed to understand that Mommy needed a bit of peace and quiet. Time to meditate and work out how we were going to keep going. After a calming meditation, I went online to try and work out how to remove the frozen egg remnants from my trailer. The news wasn't heartening. "Don't leave it on your vehicle overnight; it'll eat through the paint," one person had written. "Hold a warm soapy cloth against it for 15 to 20 minutes," another advised. Oh dear. This was going to be a mission.

I spent more than an hour scrubbing at the icy egg trails on the trailer. There wasn't any time to lose. We needed to move on through West Virginia, then on to Kentucky and Alabama for the fixing of the furnace. It was ironic that, by the time we would get the furnace fixed, we would be in warmer climes.

According to the GPS, we had only 1300kms to go to reach the Gulf of Mexico. I shivered with anticipation. I couldn't wait for the warmer weather, and the warm water of the ocean. Things were definitely looking up.

We hit the road at 10 a.m., and should have arrived at the campsite in West Virginia about four hours later. Unfortunately, the same GPS that had buoyed my mood earlier took us via the scenic route, and we only pulled up in the campsite at 7:15 p.m. I was relieved that we were able to hook up to electricity and turn on the little electric heater. I was beyond cooking, and made do with a sandwich for dinner. Toby was proving to be an absolute trooper. He entertained himself quietly a lot of the time on the road, and me (not so quietly) the rest of the time. We sang songs, loudly, and sometimes with more enthusiasm than melody, and I enjoyed pointing out interesting things along the way. Viewing the world through Toby's innocent eyes and limited vocabulary was cute, and he made me laugh often.

I looked forward to getting the furnace fixed, so that we could free camp, and I decided that, once that was done, we could slow down and take our time exploring the coast. It had been a very long day. Toby and I snuggled close under all our bedding. At only seven degrees Celsius, the little heater was struggling to make a difference to the temperature in the trailer.

The next few days passed in a blur. We spent our days on the road, and our nights at generic campsites, and I flinched every time I had to pay for camping in order to keep us from freezing to death. In Kentucky and Tennessee, we experienced temperatures as low -5 degrees Celsius, so it was a necessity rather than a luxury. It was ironic that Toby coped better with those very long days on the road than I did. Maybe because he thought about the toys he was playing with and the new things he was seeing, while I was thinking about my life: past, present, and future.

The following day, we crossed the state line into Alabama, and I couldn't resist putting on Amanda Marshall's CD and singing along to "Birmingham" as we drove through it. That's the beauty of having only a two-year-old for company. He didn't think there was anything wrong with me being myself, and I didn't have to worry about how I might be judged as cliche or sentimental. We were free. Well, I was. Toby wasn't complaining at this stage, but I was aware that I was doing what I wanted to do, and that I needed to slow down a bit for Toby. Let him have more time to run around and be a little boy.

I had a few meltdowns worrying about financing the trip, worrying about my motives for making the journey, and thinking long and hard about my lack of success in previous relationships. I even thought about my first husband, Will, and the enormous sense of guilt I'd felt at not being able to have a child for him, and at not being able to find my truth in our relationship. I had carried that burden of guilt for four years after we'd divorced. Then one day, my ever-hopeful parents had invited him to yet another family event, and I decided that I should make an effort to talk to him. I was somewhat taken aback when his first words to me after I sat next to him were, "You know, Marnie, it's actually a good thing that you left me."

"Why is that, Will?" This was one for the books. All I'd heard from him until then had been anger and recriminations.

He looked me up and down distastefully. "Because there's no way that I would EVER let a wife of mine get a tattoo, walk around with a nose piercing, and drive a truck! It's not right; what are you trying to prove?"

With that, tons of weight lifted from my shoulders. I was no longer the person who had ruined his life by divorcing him. I had given him the freedom to go out and start again, find someone more suitable, someone who didn't embarrass him. I could forgive myself. He stood up and walked away, his back stiff. I realized that he intended for me to cringe and wallow in my shame, but I didn't. For the first time, I felt free of the guilt I'd been dragging around. I liked my tattoos and my piercing, and I was incredibly proud of my achievement in qualifying as a truck driver. I was free.

I smiled at that memory. It had been a turning point in my life. How could he want me, but not accept me? People don't own other people; they choose to create partnerships because they are well-suited and love each other. Ownership is not love, and without love, fidelity is unlikely. In my mind, a partnership is an equal thing and the responsibility of both, but critical to that is acceptance of each other's good and bad points. It's important to appreciate your similarities and celebrate your differences. I don't believe that you can turn someone into your kind of person. They either are already, or they never will be.

Driving across Alabama toward Foley, Toby and I could finally peel off some of our layers. Big jackets and scarves were removed and packed in easy reach. I didn't want to be over-optimistic, but it seemed that finally, after more than 2000kms, we were reaching warmer climes. I still wasn't sure whether I was running away from the cold and society, or going in search of warmth and my own kind of people. For now, I had to just believe that it was probably a bit of both. Though I kind of wished it was more of the latter than the former. I would prefer Toby to see me as an adventurer rather than a victim.

A hundred and thirty kilometers north of Foley, just as I was starting to relax, the 'check engine' light flickered on. I groaned, and indicated before pulling over to the side of the interstate.

"What's wrong, Mommy?"

"I don't know, sweetheart. I think there's something wrong with the engine."

"Is it broken?"

"I don't know. I'm just going to take a look."

I got out of the truck and popped the hood. Things looked fine to me. Just because I had a license to drive a truck didn't make me a mechanic, though. I fiddled a bit here and there; all the wires seemed to be connected, nothing loose. I removed the air filter, cleaned it, and put it back. Then I did the same with the fuel filter. I kept looking hopefully at the passing traffic. But nobody slowed; we were buffeted by the wind from passing trucks. If I was hoping for a hero, I was out of luck.

After an hour and a half of fiddling, telling Toby that I was just fixing the problem, I eventually gave up. I couldn't find any faults. I got back in the cab, turned the key, and the engine started the first time. The warning light no longer flashed. What the hell? I'd either actually fixed the problem, or there hadn't been one in the first place. Whichever, I didn't care; it was just nice to ease back onto the road to complete our day's drive.

I don't know if Toby had picked up on my stress about the vehicle, my personal angst about what we were doing and why, or if it was just the break in routine, but that night, he decided that he was a baby again and wanted his diaper. That worried me. Was I not being sensitive enough to his needs? Was it just a comfort thing? We had changed time zones during our travels, and Toby's little body now woke at 5 a.m. and went down at 6 p.m.; that alone could be making him feel insecure. Whatever he was trying to tell me, I knew that it was time to slow down. We needed to stay put in one place for a few days and work on getting him back to his normal confident self.

Chapter 5:

From Alabama to Texas

It was a relief to roll into Foley knowing that we could settle for a while. Both Toby and I were ready for a bit of a break from the road. There was plenty to be done, I needed to get a US phone so that I could be in contact with friends and family, get the dreaded furnace fixed, and do some laundry. Make that a huge heap of laundry.

We settled into a campsite for the night, unhitched the trailer, and hooked up to the power. Toby thoroughly enjoyed playing outside while I prepared a simple dinner, and we had yet another early night. We were up early the next morning in excited anticipation of a day at the beach.

"We're going to the ocean today, Toby!"

"Yay! Ocean!" Toby did a little happy dance, and I melted inside. He was so easy to please.

He was wriggling with glee by the time I parked the truck at the beach, and I had to be quick to keep up with him once he was out. He ran onto the sparkling white sand, fine as powder. Skipped a few steps and stopped suddenly, looking down. He looked up at me quizzically, then down again. He took a firm step with his right foot, watching the sand, then dragged his left foot through it.

"What's that, Mommy?" His head was cocked as the sand squeaked beneath his foot.

"It's the sand, singing to you."

"Does it sing for you too?"

"Yes, listen."

We both listened as we walked, jumped, hopped, and skipped, creating our own little melody on the fine quartz beach. It was a beautiful moment, one of those unexpectedly simple joys that are bestowed on you out of the blue. I'd heard the sand squeak before, but never through the ears and eyes of a two-year-old. The magic he brought to ordinary experiences was beguiling.

As we entered the water the first time, Toby was splashed in the face by a small wave. He wiped it off with his hand, then licked his lips. I could see by the way his face furrowed that the cogs of his brain were turning. He lifted his hand to his mouth and sucked a finger, then dipped his hand in the water and licked at it again. His hand went back again, this time scooping up some water, which he lapped at.

"Salty!" he pronounced. "Mommy, it's salty!"

"It sure is," I laughed, "but you don't want to be drinking it; it'll make you poop."

Toby giggled and drank another handful.

"Seriously, Toby, you're gonna be sorry. Don't drink anymore."

He nodded, but I noticed that his tongue kept popping out for another lick of salt.

It was so indulgent spending a whole day playing in the sun, wading in the warm shallow waters, tracing pictures in the wet sand, skipping stones, and building castles and moats. We were so absorbed in our own imaginary beach world that I only noticed the stranger when his shadow fell across our sandy canvas. I looked up.

"Hi." He was cute. Who'd think I would meet a cute guy at the beach while doing mom-stuff?

"Hey," he responded with a grin. "Looks like fun."

"It is." I smiled. Toby nodded enthusiastically. This was definitely his best day.

"I bet I can guess where you're from."

"Okay, where?"

"Canada."

I wondered whether it was my unshaven legs after a week on the road, and quickly folded them beneath me. Flushing, I asked, "How did you guess?"

"Only a Canadian would be in a bathing suit on the beach in 74-degree weather!" He laughed.

So did I. "What? It's beautiful weather for swimming!" Toby agreed wholeheartedly.

Still smiling, he lifted a hand in salute. "Have fun." He continued his stroll down the beach.

I felt momentarily bereft. I wanted to call him back and say come and play with us. I didn't, of course, but until he'd interrupted our play, I'd been in the moment, and completely unaware that I was missing adult companionship. It took a few moments for me to get back into toddler play mode, but the spell had been broken. I felt like an adult playing at being a child. I was no longer a child with Toby on the beach; I was the supervisory parent observing him at play. I wasn't dissatisfied, but I was sorry that he'd brought that little nagging sense of loneliness to the fore of my mind.

That evening, I could have done with the cute stranger to rub some aloe on my raging sunburn. Toby, for all his fair skin, had gotten off lightly. Probably because I was more aware of his sensitive young skin than mine, and did a better job of keeping him covered in sunscreen.

I was super grateful that Toby was diaper-free because my poop warnings came to fruition, and it wasn't as funny as it had seemed earlier to poor Toby, who had given himself a full bowel cleanse with all the salt water he'd imbibed.

The sun, the ocean, and the fresh air had taken its toll on both of us, and as we shared a large bowl of spaghetti and cheese that evening, I had to make conversation to help Toby keep his eyes open long enough to fill his belly.

"What was your favorite part of today, Toby?"

"The squeaky sand... No...swimming... No...the ice cream." So many happy moments. He was absolutely spent, and I gave up trying to feed him another spoonful as his eyes drooped.

I tucked him into his bed, then sat down to fill in my journal. I thought about and wrote about the happy day we'd had. Reliving it as I wrote helped fill the hours before I would be tired enough to sleep.

The next day we packed up to take the trailer to the shop for repairs. My parents' friends, Ned and Janice, had introduced me to the gentleman who would fix our furnace. I was still unsure where we would stay while the trailer was being repaired, a hotel was definitely not in the budget. Fortunately the shop owner very kindly allowed us to stay inside his compound where other RVs that were being worked on were parked. It was kind of surreal. We had to be back inside by 5:30 in the evening and were locked in until 8:30 in the morning, when he arrived for work. The best part, though, was that it was free, helping me to get my budget back on track after the few days of having to pay for campsites with electricity.

We spent a week in Foley. I managed to get a US phone, but it would only allow me to receive calls and texts from Canadian numbers, not make them, so it wasn't ideal. It took an entire day to get all the laundry done. We seemed to have worn, used, and slept in everything we owned. I'm not a fan of doing laundry at the best of times, so I chaffed at having to write off a whole day to domestic chores; it was further complicated by Toby's energy that day. He was like a mechanical toy that had been overwound. He ran, he clambered, he got into other people's washing, and investigated every nook and cranny of the laundry room. I spent my day bouncing between the washer, dryer, folding laundry, and saving Toby from totally embarrassing us or electrocuting himself. By the time I had loaded the last of the clean laundry, I felt as tired as Toby had looked last night. I wasn't sure who would be putting who to bed. The last thing I felt like doing was cooking (or washing up afterwards), so we munched on sandwiches, then fell into bed together and I read him a bedtime story, hoping he'd fall asleep. His eyes were still open when I turned the light out, and I suspect that, despite my best intentions, I fell asleep first.

The biggest achievement in that week was getting the furnace fixed. It cost $800, though, more than half of our monthly budget. I had suspected it would be expensive, but when I pulled out my credit card to pay, my hand trembled. Who would have thought that it could be so expensive to fix a furnace?

I hated to think about what I would have paid if I hadn't had the guidance of my parents' friends. I was worried, though. I had no plan as to how I was going to pay this card off, and so far, plans of working on the road were not really panning out. We needed to settle somewhere soon so that I could try and earn money to pay this off. Although I had a credit card, I was not comfortable living on credit, and had always settled my card bills in full at the end of every month. Only, this time, it wasn't going to happen. I felt like I'd broken one of my own unwritten rules. Was I on the slippery slope of debt?

Of course we visited the beach again too, and had a few wonderful days. One particular day was marred only by the number of tar balls that we collected. We spent most of that day cleaning up 'our' beach. The turning tide had washed up hundreds of congealed balls of oil from the Deepwater Horizon oil rig that had exploded about 60 kilometers from the Louisiana Coastline in April. I was saddened by the huge mess that man had made of our beautiful oceans and beaches, all in the name of progress, and driven by greed. It was a great opportunity to educate Toby on the dangers of 'progress' to nature. My indignation was tempered by the irony of our current trip, which involved burning through tonnes of diesel. Nothing is ever quite as simple as it seems.

Once he'd gotten over the very thrilling idea of a whole big rig exploding, he warmed to the theme of environmental damage. "How much oil, Mommy?"

"Almost fifteen million liters."

He looked at me slack-jawed. "That's more than the whole ocean!"

"No. It's not. The ocean is huge, too big to measure. But it's a lot. Enough to kill hundreds and thousands of water birds and sea creatures." I struggled to find a point of reference that would help him understand the magnitude of 3.9 million barrels of oil, but failed.

His righteous indignation filled me with pride. "Why did people do that?"

"Well, they didn't mean to do it; it was an accident—a mistake. But I think it could have been avoided. You see, when you do something, it's important to think about the consequences of your actions."

He looked at me nonplussed. "What are consenses?"

Oh dear, the conversation was getting too complicated for both of us.

"Um, like, if you do something, you have to think about what else might happen. Like, if you open the truck door while I'm driving, you could fall out and get hurt."

He nodded seriously. "I wouldn't do that."

"I know. It's just an example." I was relieved when he was distracted by an older boy flying a kite. Even I struggled to grasp the enormity of the mess caused by the explosion. I was pensive, though, considering the incredible damage done. A 'mistake,' I'd called it. Actually, I thought it was more than a mistake; it was unforgivable. It should have been foreseen, and if it was still important enough to go ahead at the risk of disasters such as this, then adequate precautions and preventive measures should have been put in place. I was glad that my mistakes didn't impact the world so harshly.

Well, they did a bit. Not the world, but my immediate family. Is that what they thought when I took off on this trip? That I wasn't considering the consequences of my actions? I didn't like the way my mind was wandering, and tried to quell that line of thought. Surely how I lived my life, on my own dollar, in my own time, had no impact on them. And who was to say that the way they lived theirs was better than the way I lived mine? I sighed. It was too complicated, and I was falling into the same trap of obsessing over who was right and who was wrong. All I knew was that we were different. They did things their way and I did them my way. I'd never tried to convince my brother to get a tattoo or piercing, or even to read a book on wicca. I didn't love his values. I valued money and possessions in terms of practicality rather than status. If it wasn't serving a purpose, it wasn't necessary.

If money made him happy, wasn't it serving a purpose? I pondered. No. I decided. Definitely not. I had never seen anyone truly happy because of wealth. The more people have, the more they seem to want. It's almost as if people are programmed to be dissatisfied and striving for more. It was a never-ending cycle. I started to wonder at my own dissatisfaction, my own need to travel, to explore—was it an extension of the same problem? Did it make me different to, or more like James than I'd like to acknowledge? I stopped that train of thought right there. All I was doing was spoiling an otherwise lovely day out with Toby.

The day we left Foley, the heavens opened. The sky was as dark as evening in the middle of the morning, and traffic was slow.

Rain drummed down on the truck, faster than the wipers could clear the windscreen. I felt like I was using my whole body and mind to concentrate on staying on the road. There were times that I couldn't make out where lanes began and ended, or where the edge of the road was. I couldn't make out the markings on the road, and I drove with one foot hovering over the clutch, prepared to slam on brakes at any minute.

I was glad that the weather cleared before we drove through Mobile. It was such a wonderful experience. We crossed a bridge about 15 kilometers long, over a section of the Gulf of Mexico, then the road dipped immediately, plunging us from this scenic vista into the pitch darkness of a tunnel from which we surfaced to the brightness of Mobile before us. It was like being on a slow-motion park ride. I'm not sure who enjoyed it more, Toby or me, but when we popped out the other side, we were both grinning with exhilaration. If there wasn't still so much ground to cover ahead, I might have liked to turn around and do it all again!

We camped about 8 kilometers from the French Quarter in New Orleans for two nights, so that we could have a full day to explore. What fun! We took public transit from our campground to the French Quarter, and Toby and I rode the trolleys three times. Correction: I was informed by a friendly local that 'trolley' is an outdated term, and if I didn't want to stick out as a tourist, I should call them 'streetcars.' Whatever the name, they were a lovely experience. We swayed down the streets in these vintage streetcars, admiring the beautiful old architecture, and disembarked about four blocks from the French Quarter.

We strolled through the area, stopping to share a delicious, steaming bowl of seafood gumbo and the freshest French bread for only $3.50. It was more than enough for both of us, and if I close my eyes, I can still smell the warm yeasty bread and garlicky gumbo. It was spicy, but not hot, and left an after taste of unsweetened root beer. Quite a sophisticated flavor for someone who wasn't yet three, but Toby enjoyed it every bit as much as I did. We window shopped, Toby being far too active to risk going inside at this stage, and stopped at the French Market to sit down and listen to live band playing, for free! I loved it, and was soon swept up in the vibe. Looking to my left, I saw a middle-aged lady looking across at Toby, who was seated on my right, with a smile on her face. I turned my head to see him nodding and clapping in time with the music. Yeah! My boy had an ear for quality music. I smiled back at her, acknowledging the cuteness of the moment without words. The music went on into the late afternoon, and Toby never got bored. He was completely enraptured. I realized with some surprise that this was the first time he was experiencing a live performance.

It was hard to tear ourselves away, as the vibe picked up into late afternoon, early evening. In my pre-mommy days, I'd have stayed for sure, to experience the famous New Orleans party scene. But it wasn't to be, and Toby and I headed for home and an early night. The next morning, before moving on, I couldn't resist taking a stroll down the famous Bourbon Street, the place where I would have partied if I hadn't been on mom-duty. The stench of stale beer and vomit wafting from the sidewalk, even after the heavy rains last night, made me glad that Toby had been in charge yesterday. It's never a good idea to visit glitzy night time venues in the day; the bright sunlight makes them appear cheap and tawdry, like an aging prostitute with a hangover.

I later discovered that the area we had camped in was not the most salubrious, but what the hell? It was cheap, comfortable, and close to the action. We had felt perfectly safe.

Over the next four days or so, we covered a lot of ground. Driving all day, and camping each night in a different park, heading for Galveston, Texas. Sometimes, the long days on the road are not so good for me. I think too much. By the time we reached Galveston, I was feeling out of sorts, grumpy at the world, and the charm of the French Quarter had long worn off.

Needing to shake the cobwebs from my head when we arrived at Crystal Beach on the Bolivar Peninsula, I said to Toby, "Guess what?"

"What?"

"We're allowed to drive on the beach here!"

His eyes widened. "Are we going to?"

"You betcha!"

I couldn't wait. I put the truck into four-wheel drive and took off down the beach, not speeding, but keeping up a good momentum. A sneak peek at Toby told me he was enjoying this every bit as much as I was. Oops! I looked too long and had eased the pressure off the pedal. We were going too slow. I stopped, and fiddled with the gear. In first gear, I gently pressed down on the accelerator. The wheels spun. I released the accelerator. Damn! I checked; we were in low range, the tires should be getting traction. Another attempt and the sand flew out either side of us, and we sank another centimeter lower . I opened the door and got out. We were already sitting pretty low; if we dug in deeper, it was going to be difficult to get the truck off the beach.

"Howdy, ma'am! Looks like you're in a spot of bother."

I turned to see two men walking toward me from their truck that was stopped a safe distance from mine.

I flushed. "It seems my four-by-four isn't working." I felt guilty, like I was making excuses. But I wasn't; somehow, that just made it worse. I wasn't well suited to the damsel in distress role; there was just too much prickly pride in the way. Fortunately, these southern gentlemen saw the funny side of the situation, and after pulling my truck free of its sand trap, teased me gently about being able to drive in snow but not on sand. Realizing that the four-wheel drive was not engaging, I had to give up on our original plan, but we returned to the carpark and sat and watched the ocean while sharing a bottle of water before heading off to the ferry that would take us to Galveston.

The wait for the ferry was short, and I drove the truck and trailer onto the ferry, with Toby looking at me with utter disbelief. Parked, I got him out of the truck and we took a stroll to a good vantage point to try and spot dolphins on the 18-minute trip. We talked about the craziness of a boat being able to carry so many cars, and how, without the boat, the vehicles would sink, as we scanned the water. We saw a couple of shrimp boats, some distant tankers waiting to enter the port, and the Bolivar lighthouse fading in the distance. Then, almost simultaneously, we spotted a shiny gray shape breaking the water.

"Mom! Mom!" Toby jumped with excitement, pointing at the water, his face flushed.

"I saw. It's a dolphin! Watch carefully, we might see it again." Our efforts paid off as the dolphin gracefully sliced through the surface again before gliding back down. The ferry ride was an amazing free service, and lots of people walked onto the ferry to cross over and back again, just for fun! I was learning that there was a lot of fun to be had at little or no cost.

I was in a better mood when we disembarked; my gloom of the morning had lifted, and I was looking forward to settling into our new park that I'd booked at, just under seven kilometers from the beach. But we kept driving further. I had just started to think that I'd got the directions wrong when I spotted the entrance to the park. The park owner's idea of 7 kilometers and mine differed by about 25 kilometers. I was grumpy again.

We decided to find one that was closer. After a few calls, we did. It was definitely out of our budget, so would only be for a few nights while we regrouped. I'd booked the original park for a month. But with thanksgiving weekend coming up, our options were limited. We were about 130kms from any of the attractions I'd planned on taking Toby to. Now was not the time to be making decisions. I was feeling emotional and disappointed. Tomorrow would be better. Toby and I took a stroll on the beach, ate hotdogs, and turned in early. This was becoming a habit. I hoped that when I found our long-term place, we'd make friends and start having a bit of a social life.

I lay in bed next to my little man, calming my mind and trying to meditate. I love meditation at bedtime, when there's every chance that it can quietly slide from gentle meditation to sleep. I was just reaching that uber calm state of peace when it was shattered by blaring disco music. I leapt out of bed and stormed outside to see who the hell was destroying the peace. Across the road, neon signs blinked, and people poured in and out of what appeared to be a bar/disco. I groaned, and stomped back inside, only to doze fitfully between surges of noise. Eventually, at about two o'clock in the morning, the music stopped, and the voices started. It sounded like a hundred drunk people speaking in that overloud way that they do when they've been inside next to thumping speakers all night. I wished they'd hurry up and go away. The shouting got louder, and I peeped out the window to see a group of people, staggering and hurling insults at each other. I looked at Toby, amazed but grateful that he was still asleep.

Outside tempers were frayed, and two young men started pushing and shoving each other. Before I knew it, it was a free-for-all. Fists were flying, and they staggered *en masse*, a surge of angry, struggling boys and men egged on by shrieking girls toward our trailer, as if it didn't exist. They hit the side of the trailer with a thud, and unable to keep moving, fought up against the trailer. Even Toby couldn't sleep through that. He woke with a cry. I quickly moved away from the window, and crawled onto the bed, holding Toby tight on my lap and shushing him. He sobbed for a while, while the trailer rocked, fit to fall over. I was frozen with fear and anger. The brave part of me wanted to fling the door open and give these drunken brawlers a piece of my mind. The not-so-brave part was doing its best to pretend that we weren't there. When it didn't seem that it would ever end, I compromised, and keeping the door locked, I stood at the window and yelled loudly, using language that I'd learned in my trucking days in the Alberta oil fields. My mother would have been shocked. Certainly, Toby was; he burst into loud wails. There was a momentary silence, the rocking stopped, and the voices started to move away.

I lay down next to Toby and held him close, whispering soothing words to him as we tried to sleep, but there was too much adrenaline pumping through my veins. I must have fallen asleep eventually, though, because when Toby woke about three hours later, rested and ready for the day, I struggled to drag my eyelids open.

Exhausted, I packed up the next morning. There was no way that we could handle another night like last night. I phoned around to find a suitable place that was within budget, and had space, then drove for three and a half hours to get there. On arrival, it was obvious why they weren't fully booked at this time of the year. It was an enormous concrete lot. Not a blade of grass to be seen. I was tired and bitterly disappointed. Toby and I got out at the reception office where we were met by a self-important little cockerel of a man. He glanced over at my truck and trailer and said, "Nope, nope, you can't stay. Your units are too old." As I opened my mouth to respond, he raised one hand imperiously and said, "No use arguing; we are a respectable site, and we can't lower our standards." The polite words vanished from my mouth.

"Excuse me! I wouldn't stay here if you paid me. It looks like a parking lot, and the thought of putting up with your attitude every day—" There was a crunching sound behind me. I spun around to see Toby in the man's golf cart. He'd managed to step on the pedal and crashed into another one. As I ran toward him, to pick him up out of the cart, his face crumpled and he bawled loudly. I'm not sure it was shock or just a smart form of self-defense. But it worked. I hugged him tightly and carried him to the truck. I clipped him into his seat and then marched around to the driver's door.

"Hey! Don't you want to check the damage?" the now red-faced little man yelled.

"No, I don't! You got what you deserved." I jumped in and drove off, turning in a wide circle before spinning gravel under my wheels as we exited. I was mad. Mad. Mad. Mad. Toby was very quiet, casting anxious glances at me from time to time, but not keen to engage me in conversation. I drove for a few kilometers then pulled into a gas station parking lot to make a few calls. I found a park about half an hour's drive from where we were. And off we went again.

On arrival, I jumped out of the trailer. This looked better. Still a bit more than I'd reckoned on paying for a whole month, but I was frazzled and just wanted to settle somewhere. Toby was done with driving too, so I took him into the office with me to do the formalities. It was a woman this time. She looked us both over and said, "Oh, I'm afraid there's been a mistake. You can't stay here, it's for over 55s only."

I said between clenched teeth, "I told the lady on the phone that I had a child with me."

She flushed and stammered, "Ummm, yeah, well, ummm even so. You can't stay. Your unit is too old. We have a ten-year rule."

"Ya know what? Don't bother. I know when I'm not welcome!" I spun on my heel and found myself negotiating my way out of yet another unwelcoming campground. I drove on fuming, feeling like trailer trash. I don't know why the rejection hurt so much; it wasn't as if they were the type of people I wanted to hang out with. But just the fact that they felt in a position to judge me, my truck, my trailer, and *my child* at a quick glance, and found us wanting, incensed me. These were exactly the type of people that I didn't want or need in my life.

I drove on in indignation until I found another gas station parking lot. I pulled over. Toby was finished being quiet now, and wanted to get out and play. "No, Toby. Wait until we get there."

"Where?"

"I don't know." I wanted to cry.

"When?"

"I don't know. Just wait, okay!"

His bottom lip quivered.

"Toby, no. Please, not now." I took a deep breath, forced a smile, and gave him a kiss. "I'll get you an ice cream, okay? I'm not sure how long it'll be, but I don't want to be driving around right now any more than you do."

The ice cream did the trick. While he concentrated on getting as much of it into his mouth before it melted all over his shirt, I made a few more calls, dabbing distractedly in his direction with a paper napkin. At this stage, the truck was hot inside, I was hot, and Toby was hot. I spoke to a very calm-sounding middle-aged lady and made my inquiries.

"Yes," she said, "we can take you, but only until the first of January."

"That's fine." I responded. "Are you sure? I have a child with me."

"No problem, it's a great place for kids; we've got a playground, a heated pool, and even a duck pond."

My heart lifted slightly. "My trailer is more than ten years old."

"That's okay, dear, we don't worry about silly things like that."

"What are your rates?" Something was going to be wrong.

"$285 a month plus electricity"

"We're coming, we're coming, please don't give it away to anyone else!" I leapt into the vehicle, smiling again. Toby stared at me gravely. "We've got a place, Toby, and it's even got a swimming pool!"

He blinked, ice cream smeared around his mouth. I leaned over and gave him a noisy smacking kiss on his messy ice cream mouth and said, "Sorry I was grumpy, little man. Only half an hour and we'll be there, okay?"

He smiled. "Okay, Mommy. No more grumpy, okay?"

"No, no more grumpy."

"Good Mommy."

I blinked back the prickle of tears as his words, and turned around to drive back half an hour in the direction from where we'd come.

Ancient Oaks RV Park in Rockport, Texas was all that it promised to be, and more! They even had a mailbox for me. Only one and a half kilometers from the beach, with beautiful big trees, lovely facilities, and a super-helpful and friendly owner, I thanked my lucky stars that we'd been turned away from the other sites. It dawned on me then that far from feeling rejected, I needed to feel thankful that we hadn't been accepted into either the concrete jungle or the kid-unfriendly place. The universe had been steering us away because something better was waiting.

Chapter 6:

Settling and Unsettling

It was a relief to settle in one place for a while. For the first few days, Toby and I just enjoyed our surroundings. We spent most of our days swimming in the heated pool, which really didn't need to be heated—the weather was glorious—and playing in the playground. I couldn't believe how fortunate we had been to end up in such an idyllic spot.

On our first visit to the beach, Toby and I were taking a stroll along the pier when we passed some fishermen who were packing up their bait. Toby, with a child's natural curiosity and confidence, wandered over and looked into their livebait bucket.

"Hey, li'l fella," one of the men greeted him with a smile. Toby smiled back. "Do you want one?" Toby nodded with enthusiasm, and reached into the bucket, catching one in his little hand, and pulling it out triumphantly. It was clearly dead, which was why it had been so easily 'caught.'

"Look, Mommy!" He held his prize aloft. Then began to explore it with his hands, feeling the whole fish. He ran his little hands over its tail, and gingerly touched its eyeballs. Then wiped his smelly hand on his t-shirt.

"That's lovely, Toby, now let it go back in the water."

He shook his head, and touched its eye again. "Eyeballs."

"Yes. Eyeballs, just like yours. Now, why don't you put it back in the water?"

"It's my pet."

"It needs to go back in the water so it can find its Mommy and Daddy." I felt a bit guilty at the deception, but the idea of having a dead fish move into the trailer with us was very unappealing.

I watched the expressions play across his face as he wrestled with the decision, then he gave it a final cuddle and threw it into the water with a look of regret. "'Bye, fishy!" If he hadn't smelled like old bait, I would have hugged him.

It was very humid in Rockport, to the extent that our swimming towels took days and days to dry. Laundry was once again piling up, and I knew that sooner or later I'd have to put an end to this lovely holiday and get back on top of the daily drudge. Our site was secured until the 1st of January, after which we'd have to move the trailer to the storage site, or move on. My parents wanted us to fly home for Christmas, but that was definitely not in our already strained budget. After some calls back and forth, they insisted on paying for our flights. So, while we played in the warm outdoors, we talked about heading back to the land of snow and ice for a white Christmas.

Toby had made friends with some kids who lived there permanently, a full-timer, Guy, who was almost three, and a 10-year-old girl. Guy and Toby could play for hours. They both had toy tractors and dump trucks, and constructed roads, mountains, and mess with sand all day long. They seemed more interested in playing with each other's toys than with each other. Whatever, it kept them amused, and gave me some time to spend online trying to bolster our budget. The little girl, whose name I unfortunately don't remember, was also a full-timer. A sweet little thing, who joined us on long walks through the park on weekends, and popped over after school every day to play with Toby in the playground. She had endless patience, pushing Toby on the swing.

I didn't have as much time as Toby to make friends, but I did meet some colorful and interesting folk. One was a man who was friendly with everyone. I'll call him Dan, just to keep myself out of trouble. Dan was one of those guys who, if he was doing a beer run, would stop by the other campsites and let everyone know, so that he could pick up goods for them too. He would pop around and do repairs for some of the older folk; he always seemed to have time for everybody. His wife was more reticent, and I figured early on that she didn't like him hanging around other people, especially single women. I don't think for a moment that he had any intentions of straying, but he was very helpful to the single ladies in the park, who were most grateful for his strength and practicality. I was not keen to induce the wrath of his wife, though, so I stuck to fending for myself as much as possible.

Life was busy. On one day, I changed the truck's oil, jacked up the trailer, removed a flat tire, washed my hands, and made a snack for Toby. Then I loaded up the laundry, and when that was done, took the flat tire in for repairs and went to the bank. After leaving the bank, I picked up the repaired tire, took it home, and put it back on the trailer. By that time, Toby was bored, so I took him off for a swim, followed by a trip to the aquarium. On our return, I made lunch for Toby and me, and I was very grateful for an afternoon nap. Toby was less keen than me, but fortunately, not long after we lay down, he fell asleep, giving me the chance to do the same. I was one worn out super-mommy.

Every day was busy. If they weren't filled with chores, or online work for me, then I was filling them with adventure for Toby and me. I didn't want us to just exist. I wanted us to explore far and wide. This trip was such a wonderful opportunity to experience new things.

One day, we visited a wildlife refuge, and I was delighted to find that Toby felt a similar connection to animals as I did. I had often had meaningful dreams and visions involving animals as a younger woman, and worked with animal divination cards doing readings for friends, but these had been absent for a long time. A day or two prior to our visit to the wildlife refuge, they had returned. I had been visited by both a goose and an eagle while meditating. It felt like an omen. Goose represents migration in the fall, encouraging people to go on a quest of a journey in the fall. Reminding us that those who strike out on great quests make it easier for others to follow later on. Great quests and journeys are not always easy for the one at the head of the 'V' (you know how the Canadian Geese fly in the 'V' formation?), but the theory is that the ones who follow, follow a wise goose.

To be honest, I didn't think of myself as a wise goose; in fact, if anything, I was still a bit of a lost goose, trying to make sense of life and my place in it. But I was glad that I was at least doing something, stretching my wings and checking out the world instead of taking refuge in a safe place. The eagle visit was a bit disconcerting; in my vision, I was watching the eagle descend from the sky, talons outstretched, and it ripped my eyeballs from their sockets.

Dreams or visions of eagles are often associated with taking up opportunities, meeting your goals, and fulfilling your life. But when an eagle attacks in your vision, it can be a warning that you are about to make a risky decision, or that your courage is about to be challenged. I found these two visions conflicting, and wished that I could get a clearer meaning.

I have been interested in all things psychic all my life. As a child I knew or sensed things that others didn't. I could see things, predict things, know how the people in a room were feeling when I walked in. As I grew older, it embarrassed my family, who told me that pretending to be psychic was not endearing me to anyone. I honestly believed that I was psychic, but despite time often proving that I was right, I was told that it was all in my imagination. What I saw and understood to be real and true was not true. This was repeated often, to the extent that I began to not know what was real and what was not. It became easier to not talk about visions, and to avoid picking up feelings from other people. That in itself was difficult, and as an empath, I often felt the pain that others were experiencing. I had to try and ignore that rather than reaching out, and this brought about a guilt and pain of its own.

In my late twenties, I watched an episode of Star Trek in which Deanna Troi lost her empathic abilities, and at one point asked, "How can you people live like this?" In that moment, I realized that I had also lost something integral to my life. That episode led to me working towards gaining back my childhood accuracy, developing confidence in my abilities, and letting go of the imposter syndrome that had plagued me for years. At that stage, I had started to meditate regularly and use mantras.

On a more pragmatic note, Toby, in his enthusiasm to see the alligators at the wildlife refuge, ran ahead of me and stepped plumb into a fire ant hill. By the time I reached him, they were up his shorts and eating him alive. His tender skin was peppered with hundreds of red bites, and it didn't take long for his little leg and foot to start swelling. I tried to brush them off, but Toby couldn't stand still for a second; he was hopping and wailing with agony. "Ow! Ow! Ow! Mommeeeee!" If ever I felt somebody else's pain, it was then as I struggled to hold him still and get the little biters off him. Fortunately, help was at hand, and a park employee managed to find vinegar to douse him with. That day, I learned that, for stings and bites, including jellyfish, blue bottles, man-of-war, stingray, and fire ants, fresh water is a big no-no. Either vinegar or the hottest salt water that you can stand should be applied to neutralise the sting. I also knew for the first time that a mother really means it when she says she wishes she could take the pain instead of her child. What I wouldn't have given to have been able to spare Toby that pain.

The vinegar helped soothe the pain, and he did eventually get to see not only a huge alligator, but also the whooping cranes from Canada wintering in the USA. We might even have been close to a rattlesnake; I heard a rattle in the woods alongside the pathway, but didn't stick around to investigate. I grabbed Toby and sprinted for the truck.

On another day, we went to the beach, but the wind was blowing so hard that the sand stung my legs, and sandblasted the whole of poor little Toby. We gave up quickly and headed for home, where it was a bit calmer. That night, though, the wind reached us, and it howled all night long, massive gusts rocking the 5th wheeler. Branches cracked and crashed from the trees; leaves and sticks slapped the sides of the trailer. Everything creaked, windows and swelled and rattled, every piece of cutlery and crockery clattered and shuddered. The noise was overwhelming. We huddled inside and hoped that the trailer legs would hold out. I wondered if a hurricane was on its way. But by morning, it had passed, leaving a trail of uprooted nature and nervous people behind.

That wind left me feeling restless. We had two weeks to go before flying back home for Christmas. I was looking forward to seeing my parents, who had started to take a more positive view of my travels, my dad even sending me an article affirming the importance of children spending close time with their parents, especially children from single parent families. I couldn't say the same for seeing my brother and his family, though. I always felt a sense of foreboding before seeing them. I felt like I had to be on my best behavior, minding my Ps and Qs, and even more so Toby's. My parents had arranged for them to join us for four days. I wasn't sure that I would be able to be the person they needed me to be for that long. I was bound to disappoint and start a family row. I didn't want to, but it was almost inevitable.

I felt sorry for my mom and dad. They really wanted us to be one big happy family. I find it strange to this day that the same parents can give birth to such polar opposite children. We grew up in the same house with the same values, yet we wanted such different things from lives, our beliefs were at odds, and unfortunately, because my brother's were more closely aligned to my parents, I was the black sheep. If it weren't for the physical family resemblance, I'd have thought I was adopted. I certainly felt like an ugly and ungainly cuckoo in a nest with otherwise sleek, delicate birds.

I realized that I'd started getting comfortable with being me on this trip, and going home felt like I was going to be taking off a cool, comfortable, loose-fitting dress and forcing myself into a stiff little power suit a size or two too small for the duration. It would be fine…until the buttons burst and the real me popped out.

Speaking of buttons bursting…

In the supermarket one day, Toby called to me, "Mommy, Mommy, look! My penis is standing up all by itself!"

I whipped around to see Toby standing in the middle of the aisle, his shorts pulled down, proudly pointing at his erect penis.

I closed the gap between us in two quick strides, and said, "Uh, okay, Toby. Wow. Alright, you can put it away for now and play with it at home? It's not nice to play with it in the store. It's kind of private, okay?"

"Oh. Okay," he said, looking confused by all these funny little rules, but obligingly let me tuck it back into his pants.

A gray-haired little old lady standing nearby smiled, and said, "Well handled. I think I would have dropped my groceries and done a runner."

I smiled back. Toby was sure a learning curve for me, but I loved his innocence and lack of concern for propriety. I did, however, realize that certain things had their time and place.

Just five days before we were due to fly out to Canada, Toby got sick. He developed both a cold and an ear infection. He couldn't sleep, as every time he moved, the fluid in his ear moved, causing huge pain. He screamed with agony throughout the night, and the next morning, I had to find a doctor. Not a difficult thing in the USA, probably because being a doctor is rather lucrative. I had to pay $120 for an appointment, and the doctor's bedside manner was appalling. But it was important to get the fluid to subside before we flew. The doctor provided a prescription for ear drops and antibiotics (in case the drops didn't work). The tube in Toby's ear had also become dislodged, making him aware of a clicking sound when he swallowed. My poor boy was not a happy camper.

By the time we were packing for our family Christmas, Toby was feeling better. I was feeling low, though. My sleep had been very interrupted the last few nights. Partially because of Toby's pain, and partly because I was agonising over who I was and what I was doing with my life. I was pretty sure that this was brought on by the questions I knew I would face back home. I thought about the different people who had influenced my life. I sort of believed that everyone who comes into your life has a lesson to teach you; and that when you meet someone that you dislike, it's usually because they reflect back a part of yourself that you don't like. This was playing on my mind. I have met some people in my life who lack common sense, and some who lack basic intelligence. I wondered what part they played in my life. What lessons had they offered me?

What about the chain-smoking alcoholics? What lessons did they teach me? Maybe they were just sent to show me what my future could have been? To warn me against that way of life? If that's true, then what part of me were the chain-smoking alcoholics that I was still meeting reflecting back to me? I didn't really know. I hadn't had a cigarette now for about 15 years, and if I'd had eight drinks since leaving Canada, it was a lot. I eventually slept that night, despite a migraine, probably from trying to read too much into everyday life. Maybe some things just didn't have a purpose.

Dan had offered to take Toby and me to the airport for our flight home, for which I was grateful; it meant that I wouldn't have to worry about paying for parking for the truck. The day before we were due to leave, I was still nursing a migraine, and feeling a bit nauseous, when I bumped into him. I was confirming what time he'd pick us up when his wife, Liz, came storming over.

"What's this all about?" she asked, clearly in a foul mood.

I was a bit taken aback. She'd always eyed me with some suspicion, but I'd had little to do with her, and definitely hadn't done anything to deserve the scowl I was getting now. "Just arranging times for tomorrow," I responded.

"Just leave him alone!" she yelled, for all the world to hear. "If you can't get a man of your own, it doesn't mean you can have mine."

"Hey. Whoa! I'm not trying to steal your man. Just getting a lift to the airport."

"Yeah, that's what you say now. I wasn't born yesterday. We don't need people like you around here."

"What do you mean by 'people like me?'"

"You know exactly what I mean. I don't need some slut hanging around sniffing after my husband."

That word! A red mist blurred my vision. "Don't you dare!" I spluttered. "You don't know the first thing about me!"

"I know more than I want to. Just fuck off and leave my husband alone. You're a whore!"

"You bitch!" My eloquence had deserted me.

"I might be one, but at least I'm not the one sleeping around."

"Neither am I!"

"Yeah? Where's Toby's father then? I know your kind. You just use men. I'm watching you."

"Toby's father is none of your business. You don't know the first thing about me. And if you have trust issues with your husband, maybe you should take a good look at yourself." I turned to Dan. "Thank you for offering, but your wife doesn't trust you and I don't need her type in my life. So, thanks, but no thanks. I'll make my own way there."

I spun on my heel and walked home, angry tears blurring my vision. I could hear her still shrieking like a fishwife, but was too absorbed in my own indignant hurt to make out what she was saying. I had no romantic interest in Dan whatsoever. I thought he was a nice guy, always helpful. But he did far more favors for the elderly ladies around the park, taking them shopping, carrying stuff for them, than he ever did for me. What the hell did me, for once, accepting a favor from him, have to do with my sex life? I could have howled at the unfairness of it. What sex life? Shit. We were flying tomorrow, and now had no lift to the airport. I had to stop wallowing in self-pity and start solving the immediate problem.

After a few phone calls, I hastily grabbed the last of our things together and loaded them into the truck. I'd found a hotel near the airport that offered free parking if you stayed the night before your flight. Toby and I had to get going today in order to qualify. Poor Toby. Everything was upside down again.

I tried to put a positive spin on it. Talking about what fun it would be to sleep in a hotel. It was a treat, a great adventure. I struggled to maintain the enthusiasm, though, my mind constantly inspecting that slut label. I couldn't help trying to see myself from an outsider's perspective. What made people think I was loose. Was I too friendly? Did I wear my clothes too short or my tops cut too low? I did wear a bikini when I swam, but this was the 2000's damnit, not the 1800's. Most women wore bikinis. I dressed more for comfort than for show, lots of jeans and t-shirts. Was it my nose piercing, or my tattoos? Surely in this day and age people didn't judge others for having body art?

Maybe I was just too honest. Maybe I should have told people that Toby's father was dead, and I was widowed. No. I couldn't do that. Toby hadn't asked about his dad yet, and I didn't want to live a lie, and I didn't want to lie to Toby. I wasn't sure yet how I was going to answer those questions, but I knew it would at least have to be some version of the truth. I smarted all the way to the hotel, then decided that I couldn't be held responsible for Liz's insecurities. That was Dan's problem, not mine. It was nearly Christmas, and it was going to be Toby's first 'real' Christmas; the first two he'd been too young to appreciate the magic of it. I wanted it to be special; that would be tough enough given my fragile relationship with my brother and his wife without dragging Liz's hurtful words along with me.

That night, after Toby had fallen asleep, I took advantage of the hotel's free Wi-Fi to go online and check my bank balance. The visit to the doctor and now the hotel bill, on top of the cost of the furnace repair, were stressing me. I had no idea how I was going to make my card payment at the end of the month, and I still needed to do some Christmas shopping. What a horrible mess.

Something wasn't right. In my account was a deposit of $800 with a reference that meant nothing to me. I looked at it again, unable to believe my eyes. It must have been a mistake. I checked the balance of my account, just to make sure it was a credit and not a debit. Yup. My balance had increased. By exactly the amount we would need to get the furnace repaired. I even checked that I hadn't accessed somebody else's account in error. Nope. It was my account. But was it my money? I was too scared to use it in case somebody came looking for it.

A few calls the next morning cleared up the mystery. The courts had finally caught up with Jacob and garnished his salary. After more than two years. On the day that I had no idea where to find the money to keep going, I had received almost the exact amount it had cost to repair the furnace. If that wasn't a sign, I'm not Marnie McBain. My mood instantly revived, and I whooped with glee. It wasn't going to make me rich, and the way Jacob job-hopped, it probably wouldn't continue for very long. But right now—it was exactly what we needed!

Toby and I left for the airport in a positively festive mood. Maybe the universe was making up for yesterday's misery.

Toby's excitement at flying in an airplane was infectious. We held hands during take off and landing, and I was glad that his ear was better. I gave him some chewing gum to help with the change in air pressure.

My migraine had cleared, and I was feeling physically strong, but emotionally fragile. My stomach fluttered with nerves. I had a job interview lined up back home. It wasn't the interview that was worrying me so much. It was more of a formality than an actual interview. It meant committing myself to going home, and settling down to a daily grind. It would definitely help financially, but somehow, I couldn't get past the feeling that I was selling my soul. I couldn't imagine condominium management setting my soul free. I didn't dislike it, and knew I was good at it, but there's a difference between being good at something and really enjoying doing something. I know life is hard, and everyone has to choose their own 'hard.' Life can't be all moonlight and roses. I'm realistic enough to understand that every job has its ups and downs. I just wished I could shake this feeling that I was giving up on my dream. What dream? Here I was, over 40 and trying to work out what I wanted to be? Oh dear. I might have learned to be a mom on this trip, but it appeared that I still hadn't gotten to know myself. Ah well, I thought, I didn't have to commit immediately. The job wasn't due to start until the end of February, and I was hoping to negotiate an even later start date around late April or early May. I wasn't quite ready to give up on our travels yet.

Chapter 7:

The End of the Journey

It was wonderful to see my parents. I was shocked to discover that the day before I'd arrived home, my mother had had an accident. She'd ended up in a ditch with her car written off. She was fine, several bruises and a bit stiff, but otherwise her chipper self. She said her pride was more hurt than her body. Toby was fascinated by the account of Grandma's accident, and when we went sledding the following day, he was determined to try and recreate a sled version of it.

There was a whirl of pre-Christmas preparations, shopping, visiting, and catching up with friends, in between throwing snowballs and fun. There were snowmobiles on the lake, and we were excited for my brother's arrival on Christmas day; my Dad and I had cleared a skating rink on the ice, and James would be able to help with flooding it to get a smooth glass-like surface.

The job interview went well. That wasn't unexpected. But I was still torn about what to do. Give up our itinerant lifestyle? Or give up on the job offer? To be honest, finances were very tight, so taking the job would be the practical option. It felt like a big step backward, though, and traitorous to myself. I wasn't sure I was ready to settle yet. I wasn't sure if I ever would be. I put off making the decision.

This was going to be my best Christmas ever. I felt Toby's excitement as we put out cookies and milk for Santa. He was keen to jump into bed and be a good boy for Santa, but struggled to fall asleep. Too much anticipation. I had to read him three stories before his eyes finally drooped and he nodded off. As soon as he was safely asleep, I tackled the gift wrapping. So many gifts, I'd completely blown my budget in my enthusiasm. I couldn't wait to video him opening his presents under the tree the next morning.

I woke at six o'clock, as usual, and stretched in the bed. Something was wrong. The house was too quiet. I tiptoed over to Toby's room and watched his chest rise and fall gently as he slept on in all his innocence. I marvelled at the sheer perfection of this child. My boy. I decided not to wake him, because there were still hours to go until my brother and his family arrived. It was going to take an enormous amount of persuasion to keep him from opening his gifts before his younger cousins arrived.

I was sitting in the living room when he woke about half an hour later. I heard the slap of his running feet before I even saw him. He skidded around the corner, taking it a bit wide, eyes bright and cheeks flushed. He launched himself onto my lap, wide-eyed. "Did Santa come, Mommy?"

"He sure did!" I scooped him up into a snuggle. I loved those early morning snuggles when he was still soft and warm from bed, but he was having nothing of it. He wriggled with excitement, bumping my chin with his head.

"Did he bring presents?"

I bit back my smile. "He did."

"For me?"

I nodded, unable to stop the beam on my face as he yelled, "Yes! Yes! Yeahhh!"

"What's all this noise?" My mother and father ambled into the living room, smiling broadly, still wrapped in their bathrobes.

"Santa came! Santa came!" Toby sang out, squirming off my lap and throwing his arms around my mother.

"Wonderful! Happy Christmas, everyone!" my father said with a wink, as he leaned down to give me a kiss and ruffled Toby's hair. "I never doubted that he would."

"Which is mine, Gramma?" Toby asked, tugging at my mom's hand.

"Oh, I'm not sure. We'll have to get Mommy to read the cards and figure it out. But you're going to have to be a good boy for a while. We have to wait for Travis and Carter before we can open them."

"Didn't Santa go to their house?" Toby looked worried for his cousins.

"I'm sure he did," Grandma replied, "but there are presents here for them too. Now come, I've got some lovely cookies and some milk for you in the kitchen—just like the ones you put out for Santa. Let's go get them!" Toby went with her, but the look of longing on his face as he glanced back over his shoulder at the gifts under the tree made my heart ache.

"Don't worry, little man. They'll be safe here; I'll take good care of them."

As the hours passed, and I played with Toby outside, and got him to 'help' with the food inside, my frustration grew. Poor child. He kept sidling off to the living room and eyeing the prettily-wrapped packages under the tree. It was getting hard to think up new ways of distracting him.

At 11 a.m. when James and family were already two hours late, I eventually caved in and gave Toby one of his presents. It was from Santa and hadn't been wrapped, because I'd gotten carried away and bought too many. I'd thought I'd give it to him when we got back to the USA, but I couldn't leave him hanging all day. Not after all the excitement and build up the previous evening. I was starting to feel annoyed at James. I should have anticipated it, though. They had arrived late the previous year too. It was just worse this year because Toby understood and anticipated so much more. I felt guilty for having been party to his excitement, only to let him down on the day.

By the time James and his family arrived, it was 4 p.m., and I found it difficult to fake smiles and happiness. Toby was exhausted from a long day of busy distraction, and dinner was almost ready.

"Sorry we're late!" James called out as they came in through the front door. "It took ages to open all our gifts, and then Travis needed to play with everything before we could get going!"

Travis rushed in behind him, waving his toys in the air, showing off his morning's loot. I hugged and kissed them all, trying to hide my annoyance. My eyes kept turning to Toby lying on the couch listlessly. It was too late; the magic was gone.

Toby barely held out for dessert before asking if he could go to bed; the gifts would have to wait for morning. I lay awake in an angry snit long after everyone had retired to bed. I felt bad about being so annoyed. My parents had been very good to us, and I had been happy to have the opportunity to fly home for the holidays. But I was so disappointed for Toby that all I wanted to do was get out of there. I dreaded the pretense of the next four days. I was fully aware that I irritated my brother and his family every bit as much as they did me, and that our discord worried my parents. I lay awake thinking about how to change the situation. I told myself that change comes from within, and that I would need to change my attitude, practice gratitude, and embrace the positive in order for the universe to align and effect change. The problem was that I was having a hard time getting past the negatives that were doing a fine job of hiding the positives.

Well, we made it through the family Christmas without any obvious fallout. I can't say that either Toby or I bonded with my brother and his family, though. I guess the kids were too young to form any kind of meaningful relationship, and Toby, being the eldest, albeit by a hair's breadth, took the brunt of any adult censure over the sharing of toys. I wanted to scream every time I saw the look of puzzled hurt on his face as he got chastised by my brother and his wife. My parents tried to stay as neutral as possible.

We flew back to Rockport and retrieved the truck from the hotel on the 28th of December. Fetching the trailer from it's storage site in the early evening, I was walking toward it with Toby when a searing pain tore through my foot. I yelled, frightening the living daylights out of poor Toby. Looking down at the offending foot, I spotted an angry scorpion, pinchers outstretched and tail arched. Damn! I must have stood on him in my flimsy flip-flops, and he'd zapped me. I lifted Toby onto my hip and headed inside, where I tried dabbing the red patch with vinegar. Within 10 minutes, my foot and leg were swollen, all the way up to my knee. The pain was intense, and burned its way right up my leg and into my lower back. Toby was very concerned.

"Are you okay, Mommy?"

"I'm sore, little man, but I'll be okay," I said.

"Make it better."

"I am. It'll get better soon."

"Good. It's a naughty scorpion."

"Not really. It was doing the only thing it knew how to protect itself. It must have gotten a huge fright when I stepped on it. Look how big I am and how small the little scorpion is."

He shook his head and planted a sweet little kiss on my foot. "It should have got out the way."

I slept fitfully that night with a raging headache and flu-like aches throughout my body, but by the time we woke the next morning, the general body aches were gone; the headache continued to pound for three days, but the swelling on my leg had reduced and only the localised pain still stung with a general burning sensation. The scorpion had found a soft target in the arch of my sole.

On New Year's Eve, I sat and watched Toby sleep his sleep of innocence, and mulled over how much he had changed my life.

In previous years, I would have joined the fray celebrating all night long and waking with a hangover. Did I miss that? No. I decided that I didn't. New Year's celebrations were overrated. There was always a sense of bitterness and disappointment, and the subsequent hangover usually just amplified the crappiness of the previous night. I wasn't sad; I was more regretful of the changes that I hadn't made. The things I hadn't had the courage to say or do.

I did have a whiskey, two in fact, as I sat and watched over Toby. I reflected on the previous year. I thought of how lucky I had been to be able to spend so much time with him. I contemplated how to continue to support myself and my boy without giving up my soul to a job that wasn't me. I tried to figure out how to grow spiritually. I meditated and decided that this was what I'd focus my energy on in 2011. Trying to find a way forward that worked for both me and Toby. For the first time in many years, I didn't cry myself to sleep on New Year's Eve.

We left Rockport on New Year's day and drove for hours through desolate desert, heading in the direction of Fort Stockton. On the map, the town looked a reasonable size, but actually only had a population of 8,000. With only about 11 kilometers to go, the truck stopped dead, smoke pouring from the engine. I leapt out and threw the hood open, panicked that the whole thing was about to catch alight. As I did so, the heat and hissing alerted me to the fact that this was steam, not smoke.

Thank goodness we had cell phone signal, albeit sketchy; I called for help. I thought of my parents who'd nagged me about three weeks back to purchase tow insurance for the truck and trailer. Thank goodness I'd listened to them!

The tow truck pulled the truck and trailer in tandem to a repair garage, an impressive sight to behold. The owner was an elderly chap, tanned, gnarled, and gray, with light blue eyes that creased from years of laughter and squinting into the sun. He and his wife were amazing. They not only allowed us to camp in their parking lot while they arranged for the necessary parts to travel nearly 250 kilometers from the nearest major center, but they ran hydro and water out to the trailer. They let us shower in their home, and even lent me their own truck to go grocery shopping.

Grocery shopping brought its own challenges. In the middle of the desert, vegetables are few and far between. What you can find is either wilted and manky or very expensive. Everything was expensive. I had, on the journey so far, paid an average of $3.00 per gallon for fuel. In Fort Stockton it was $3.49.

While I stressed over finances, Toby enjoyed every adventure. Even when we broke down, and the trailer shuddered every time a transport truck passed by. He was having the time of his life. I was all his, and he entertained both me and the lovely couple who had been so kind. The carpark of the garage didn't seem to him to be a strange place to play. I wished I could feel as carefree as he did. My credit card was going to have to be called upon again for an unexpected hit to the finances.

Well, in for a penny, in for a pound. While I had the wisdom of the garage owner, I asked him if he could help me find a used generator in reasonable condition. It was another big expense, but in the long run, it would mean that we could be completely self sufficient and take advantage of more primitive (and affordable) campsites.

As soon as the truck was ready, and the generator purchased (for $400!), Toby and I went to visit Carlsbad Caverns in New

Mexico's Guadalupe Mountains. It was stunning with amazing rock formations, stalagmites and stalactites extending from the roof and floor of the cave. The biggest cavern, called the Big Room, was a limestone cave about 750 feet underground— roughly the size of 6 football fields. Toby was very quiet and awed by the caves, and stuck close to me every step of the way. Finally, we'd found something that he didn't just take in stride. He was most fascinated by a broken ladder leading to a lower cavern. "Do you think someone fell off it when it broke?" he asked, looking worried. This bothered him for most of the day, and he kept checking if I was sure that nobody had been hurt.

The National Park was fantastic. We'd initially only planned a one night stopover, but there was no light for kilometers around, making the night sky an enchanting canopy of stars. We also met a very interesting man, David, and his daughter, who were camped there. We ended up staying a second night. David, his daughter, Toby, and I went out for dinner together, then met up again the next day to go to the farmers market, after which we walked in the park and had lunch together. I was fascinated by David, a kindred spirit. He owned a ranch in northern New Mexico, which he one day hoped to convert into a sustainable living community. Like me, he believed that the world was on the brink of major change. Not as some believe a cataclysmic disaster, just major change. We spoke at length about how people were going to have to be more adaptable in order to survive the natural changes that were in the cards.

We were sad to say goodbye to David and his daughter, but for the first time since leaving home, we were bound to a schedule. We were meeting up with my parents at an RV rally in Quartzsite, Arizona. It was an interesting annual event. The city itself was home to only about 3,000 people, but for a six-week period over January/February, it swelled to over a million when it became a massive farmer's market, with vendors from all over the globe. Even more exciting than the abundance of fresh vegetables was the fact that rocks, gems, and fossils from all over were sold there. I couldn't help thinking that I'd find some like-minded hippies there.

We stopped in Nogales and parked the trailer in a Wal-Mart car park. Nogales is a town in Arizona, on the edge of the Mexican border. I was fascinated by the fact that you could just walk across the border and you'd be in another town, also called Nogales, only in Mexico. Toby and I did just that. We locked up the trailer in the parking lot and walked to the border post. We weren't stopped for any formalities. Nobody wanted to check our IDs or passports. Nobody even spoke to us until we entered the town: there, a few men offered to show us around the town for a fee. They explained that that's how they fed their families. I sympathised, but our budget wasn't up to guided tours.

I wondered once or twice about the wisdom of going into Mexico, just Toby and me. It was quite eerie. Within 100 meters of each other were two towns with the same name, but nothing else in common. The wealth, bravado, and in-your-face advertising lining the clean streets of Nogales, Arizona versus the dusty, cracked streets and sidewalks on the Mexican side was remarkable. The streets were suddenly narrow, and windows either broken or boarded up.

We didn't venture too far, because I felt spooked, and given the poverty and desperation, I was on edge and turning at every sound. I felt more comfortable when we got back to the border. Departing Mexico was one thing, but entering the USA was quite another. We had no stamps in our passports; when I was asked for our address in the USA, I'd pointed to the trailer over the way and said, "We're camping in the Wal-Mart parking lot." I guess a single mom and her toddler walking into a cartel town for a few hours did come across as mighty suspicious. It took four hours of being grilled before they let us through. I later discovered that Nogales, Mexico is a cartel town, and it was likely that the border officials suspected I might be a drug mule.

The next day, Toby and I drove through Tucson, Arizona. All of the flags were flying at half-mast following the tragic shooting of 19 people at a constituent meeting in the parking lot of a Safeway store the previous week. Now, only about a week later, huge posters and banners announced the National Rifle Association's gun convention that was taking place. I shuddered at the irony and insensitivity of it all. I sometimes think the world would be a better place if firearms had never been invented.

Arriving in Quartzsite was an eye opener. The town only has about 300 motel rooms, so there were RVs as far as the eye could see. The free camping was dry and very basic. No water, no sewer hook-ups, no electricity. But it was free. Entrepreneurial townsfolk had developed big septic tanks and water tanks on their properties, where they charged RV owners an extortionate price to 'dump and fill.' I was glad of our generator, though I limited the use of it, aware of the sound and environmental impact. I looked forward to solar energy becoming more affordable and commonly available.

Toby and I had the good fortune of being camped alongside a wonderful nomadic family. They were living my dream, traveling pretty much full-time. They supported themselves by making jewelry and busking. One of them was a mechanic who picked up jobs where he could. These were the free and easy-going, sociable, generous type of people I'd been craving to meet! We had a dirty, minimalistic, but happy-go-lucky couple of days, washing out of buckets and living free. Both Toby and I were in our element.

When my parents arrived, we met up with them and camped with them for a few days. The arrival of my parents coincided with a complete change in Toby's behavior. It was like a switch had tripped. The good, caring, gentle child I had been traveling with had disappeared, and in his place was a wild man. He ignored every word I said, and worse, ignored my parents too. He refused his afternoon naps, and by early evening on the first day, was so out of control that we had to hold him down to settle him. I'd never seen this kind of obnoxious behavior from him before, and it really threw me.

Thankfully, after a couple of days, Toby morphed back into himself—for a day or two. I didn't know if his unusual behavior had been sparked by a need to show off in front of his grandparents, or petulance at having to share my time with them, but it had been quite frightening to experience. Three days later, my mom and dad left for Phoenix for about 10 days, while Toby and I stayed on in the desert before heading to Yuma to meet up with them again.

In the time that Toby and I spent alone in Quartzsite, I saw more of the type of behavior he'd displayed earlier. He became more and more active and more and more demanding of my time and attention. He became defiant, challenging me and frustrating me. Tantrums were a regular thing, and my fuse became very short. I started yearning to be somewhere else, but where? I didn't know. The free camping was handy, but the average age of the campers was about 68. By those standards, I was young! I figured that Toby needed other children to play with, and that I was struggling to fill that gap. I was all played out, and exhausted from chasing and being responsible for a little one tearing and screaming for attention 24/7. I felt a desperate need to stop being a parent and be an adult for a while.

I realized that what I was seeing was Toby entering his terrible twos. The place and the company probably had little to do with it; it would have happened anyway. It didn't help that this transformation coincided with my approaching birthday (about which I had mixed feelings), or that it came at a time when I was so conflicted about our future. I was struggling to decide whether it was time for me to take up the condominium job that was due to start in about two months' time, or not. I was dreading putting Toby into day care full-time, and dreading doing something that felt meaningless to me. I hadn't yet found what I was looking for on our journey, but I also needed to be practical. Maybe settling for a while and taking a normal job would help me save funds and plan our next journey. I felt a pull to travel more widely, to go further afield than North America. I wanted to meditate and write down my hopes and dreams, create a visualization. Toby wanted me to run, dig, and play. We were at odds, but as the adult in the relationship, I had to consider his needs as well as mine. I gave up joining him for his afternoon naps, and instead used that as my contemplation time.

One night, I dreamed about going back to work. In my dream, I arrived for my first day. Everyone appeared happy to see me and were going through all the right welcoming motions, but it felt fake and forced; I sensed underlying unhappiness. They told me that they had their own day care for an employee's children and directed me to take Toby down the hall and outside. I walked down a long, narrow hallway then out into a large area that looked like a zoo. There were many animals there and pathways leading between them. I didn't like the feeling of it at all, but other employees kept reassuring me that it was safe, the animals were tame. So, I left Toby reluctantly and headed back into the building. Within minutes, I knew that something was terribly wrong, and I sprinted back to the child care area.

I saw a lion chasing Toby around, and sprinted toward him. Before I could get there, the lion grabbed him by the seat of his pants and started running off. I could feel both my fear and Toby's coursing through my veins. I ran so fast it felt like I was going to overbalance. I eventually caught up with the lion and snatched Toby from his mouth.

The lion looked at me with guilt in its eyes and silently communicated that he was sorry, he was only doing what was expected of him. I turned to leave with Toby, and my new colleagues chased after me, saying they were sorry, and asking if I would be back the next day because they didn't want to lose the contract.

I woke in a sweat, my heart thumping fit to bust. All I could think was that nobody had cared about me or Toby; their only concern was the contract.

The day after the dream, a woman at the Pow-Wow Rock and Gem Show, completely out of the blue, looked me in the eye and said, "When are you going to join the healers and light-workers? You know this is your path and journey. You've known for a long time. Now is the time to heal! You've done your work; now is the time to share, teach, and heal others. You have an uncanny ability to show others their inner positives when they can't see them themselves."

I looked at her for a moment, wondering if she'd mistaken me for someone that she knew. "Do I know you?"

She shook her head dazedly. "I'm sorry, that wasn't me. We haven't met. It was my spirit guide." She looked at me in wonder. "You know, that's only the third time that's ever happened to me."

The next night, we saw the most incredible moon-rise. It looked like something out of a Hollywood movie. It was two days after the full moon as it began to wane. It was still light enough to see in the desert without a flashlight. The sky was almost cloudless as the moon slid up into the sky over the mountains, only three kilometers away. Around our communal campfire, it was agreed that it was definitely a moon indicating change on the horizon. Lively conversations ensued about what type of change to expect. A simple change in the weather? Or was this indicative of greater change?

It left me thinking. Toby was experiencing change and growth, as he developed both physically and intellectually. He was developing opinions and emotions, but could not yet express them clearly. This was the root cause of his frustration. I was on the cusp of change, but unsure about the right path,both for me and for Toby. If I wasn't a parent, the correct route would be easier to identify, but our needs were different, and it was my responsibility to balance both.

After this, I became much more aware of things that weren't as they seemed. I was aware of the contrasts between the materialistic and minimalistic people that I met, and could see stark differences between people who genuinely cared, and those who were all fake smiles and facades. I wondered whether it was the desert that had brought about this clarity? Or was it the moon? Maybe it was the people with whom I was keeping company? I thought of my suppressed childhood visions and wondered whether I was an impostor, playing at being psychic, or if this was the real thing.

My natural, unworldly ability to believe had been tempered by skeptics over the years. Somewhere, deep down, I did still believe in psychic powers. But did I have them? Or did I only wish I had them, or fantasize about having them? I didn't feel that I could work as a psychic. What if I was an impostor? What if I was just deluding myself and hearing what I wanted to hear? Seeing what I wanted to see?

A few days later, I received an email from my old friend Dee who had been following my blog posts. She told me that she thought I needed to do more research to find like-minded people who accepted kids. She even suggested looking into a community in Auroville in India. It was funny, I had thought about visiting India before, but always came up with too many reasons not to. Now I wondered if these were reasons or excuses?

We traveled via Kofa Wildlife refuge, where I had hauled out a drum my parents had bought me from the Tarahumara Indians in Northern Mexico some years back. I hadn't played it much because it had always sounded like the skins weren't stretched enough, or dry enough. But Toby insisted that I play it for him at sunset that night in Kofa, and the sound was perfect; a deep, hollow, haunting sound. It was probably just the lack of humidity, but I liked the notion that it played better closer to its origins. That night, a pack of coyotes sniffed around the trailer after Toby had gone to bed.

We met up with my parents in Yuma as planned, but our trip with them through Palm Springs, Desert Palm, and Indio, California fell through when my father's brother, Uncle Byd, took a turn for the worse with his cancer and was admitted for palliative care. They put their motorhome in storage, to be collected sometime in the future, and rushed home.

Toby and I stayed on, waiting for new tires for the trailer before we could move on safely. We visited Mexico again, more for the food than anything else. This time we crossed into a town that catered specifically to American's and had not yet been affected by the drug cartels. There I discovered that I could have my teeth cleaned cheaply, and I even bought two pairs of prescription glasses (including frames and transition lenses) for only $140. Toby had a bout of nausea and diarrhea, which added to our laundry pile, but fortunately didn't last too long. The business of Yuma was overwhelming after the peace of the desert, and with my budget and the truck and trailer covered in sand, neither our units nor children were welcome in the snooty RV parks. I suppose we were looking a bit worse for wear. No matter how hard I scrubbed, I kept finding new deposits of sand everywhere.

Once the new tires had arrived and been fitted, Toby and I headed to Castle Dome Ghost Town and Museum. A little ghost town in the middle of nowhere that was being refurbished as a tourist attraction. It had started as a silver mining town, then in World War II, they switched to mining the hills for lead before returning to silver after the war. The town had been abandoned in the 1970s, when the price of silver had tanked. It was like walking onto a movie set for an 1800s spaghetti western. Only it was real. I could imagine a gunfight in the streets, people spilling out of the saloons to be in on the action.

I was sad to hear that Uncle Byd lost his battle with cancer a few days later and passed over to the other side. I was glad that my parents had flown home when they did and were able to say goodbye and be there for the arranging of the funeral.

Without my parents there, and feeling quite unwelcome in the town, I turned back to Quartzsite. We overnighted at Imperial

Dam, where we swapped dry, dusty sand for sticky mud. Toby enjoyed playing in the mud around the reservoir, until his foot got stuck deep in it and he couldn't get out. I had to pull him out, and spent half an hour trying to get the mud off our legs, only to have him dart right back out for more.

Back at Quartzsite, Toby and I had endless entertainment. One Sunday afternoon, we came across a man who walked on fire and broken glass, bent a bar with his neck, and broke bricks with his bare hands. He was fascinating. He'd been shot in combat and spent months in a coma. After coming out of the coma, he suffered from amnesia and did not realize his parents or his wife, nor have any memory of his life. He was paralyzed and expected to never walk again. He regained his ability to walk through energy healing with the laying of hands. He was looking for volunteers to walk across his fire pit, and there were none forthcoming. I had done a fire walk once before, and was keen to try it again, so I stepped up.

To be honest, I did get 'bit' by this fire a couple of times, unlike my first fire walk. There are a couple of theories as to why people get 'bit' by the fire. One, is if you're not mentally prepared for the walk, which might have been my case. I'd had to leave Toby while I did the walk, and he wasn't impressed at being held back by a stranger, which was distracting for me. The other theory is that you only get 'bit' in the area of your foot that reflexologists relate to specific organs. I was 'bit' in several places associated with my colon, stomach, and sinuses. I wasn't surprised. I'd been eating meat again, and it was wreaking havoc on my digestive system. As for my sinuses, after all the time in the dust and dryness of the desert, my sinuses were giving me hell. It was worth the walk, though; I was on a natural adrenaline high that lasted long into the evening.

From there we traveled to Lake Havasu City for the International Pyrotechnics Competition. Our trailer was perfectly situated for the displays, which started every evening at 7 p.m. and continued for three hours. Toby was startled at first by loud booms, cracks, and sizzles, but soon learned to watch for the exciting sparkles that sprayed across the sky afterwards. His face was a picture. I probably spent more time looking at him than I did at the actual display. Toby loved Lake Havasu, although we were free camping in the desert. There was a park nearby that even featured a wave pool and toddler water slides. It did make it easier for me, that there was entertainment laid on, and I wasn't having to think up games in the sand. BUT, with more people and the water to be concerned about, I started to feel that I was stuck in permanent babysitting mode.

That I loved Toby was never in question, and I wasn't actively looking for a partner, but I missed having a person that I could have adult conversations with, share my concerns and my dreams and hopes, and yeah, a little help with the chores and child care would have been nice too. The weather turned cold and wet, and so did my mood. The thought of returning to work was weighing heavily on me. I started to truly envy those who knew from childhood what they wanted. The kids who at school said, "I want to be a fireman, or nurse," or whatever. Here I was, all grown up, raising a child of my own, and feeling so lost. I didn't know what I wanted to be. When would I ever know what would truly make my heart sing?

With only two months to go before we had to head back to Canada, I decided to explore Joshua Tree National Park. Driving up into the mountains, temperatures dropped further with the elevation, and Toby, lulled by the movement and snuggled against the cold, fell asleep, giving me time to reflect.

I realized that sometime, shortly after Christmas, I'd lost sight of the purpose of this journey and it had become a destination. I was viewing it from the wrong perspective. This was a journey, and the destination ultimately was the building of a relationship, a bond between Toby and me. The destination was not Ontario, or Alberta, or selling the truck and 5th wheel to make sure I'd have enough money for a car. Even the job was not the be all and end all; it was just a tool to help me on my journey.

Yes, the terrible twos are a natural phenomenon, but I wondered whether my continual stressing about the future hadn't harmed Toby's journey. My emotional roller coaster over the past two months probably contributed to creating the screaming, fussy, mouthy two-year-old. I realized that I needed to pull myself together and break the habits of snapping and yelling. It was up to me to respond more positively to this difficult and frustrating period of his life.

Of course, that was easier thought than done. Once we were settled, and Toby was up to his tricks again, I discovered just how difficult it was going to be to make these changes. Sometimes, it was as if he was deaf, flatly ignoring me until I freaked out. Sometimes, when he was really hurting me, I'd tell him calmly and ask him to stop, but then he'd just go right on doing it, again and again, until I yelled. I hadn't fully considered or anticipated how difficult it could be to be one-on-one with a small child for such an extended period. I'd counted on meeting travel companions along the way who would share advice and become a part of my 'tribe.'

We loved the ancient rock formations of the park; at a distance, they could be mistaken for large sand dunes, but they were granite that had aged and become crumbly. Toby loved the Joshua Trees (or Yucca Palms) that the park was named after.

They looked very different from the trees we knew in Canada, spiky, with 'arms' raised heavenwards, and resembled to my mind the offspring of a palm tree and cactus. We saw a wood rat, which was surprisingly squirrel-like, as well as lots of desert hares and coyotes.

After a week in the park, we left to meet my parents in Slab City, California. It was originally a military base, Camp Dunlap, but had been renamed after the many concrete slabs that were left behind when it was abandoned in 1956. Although Camp Dunlap had boasted roads, sewage systems, and water, none of that remained. It was now effectively a squatter camp. One that I suspect the government would rather just forget about. The population: a combination of permanent squatters, itinerant squatters, and campers. The permanent 'residents' referred to themselves as 'Slabbers,' and the visiting campers as 'Normies.' I found it funny being referred to as a 'Normie.' My brother, I'm sure, would have found it hysterical. It seemed I just really didn't belong anywhere, but what's that expression? In the land of the blind, the one-eyed man is king?

My parents were not as charmed as I was. To be honest, I could understand why. While some of the campers and squatters kept their patches clean and tidy, others made no effort, leaving garbage lying around in a disgusting mess and living like pigs. While I wasn't crazy about the filth in certain areas, I was fascinated by the eclectic mix of colorful, cool, and uncommitted characters I met there, and couldn't wait to go back and get to know them better. I say 'uncommitted' because many of them were free spirits, unfettered by alarm clocks, phones, TVs, and the constant barrage of media hype. They were committed to each other, karma, and of course, survival. Their priorities were so different to the masses that populated the towns, offices, and suburbia that most of us grew up in and aspired to emulate.

After my parents left, Toby and I stayed on with the 'rainbow' people of Slab City for about three weeks. I watched Toby play with other rainbow kids, getting dirtier and dirtier, and happier and happier. I shared food with other rainbows, and they shared with me. We discovered a (somewhat muddy) hot spring that we soaked in, and one night, I even took Toby to a movie. It was an outdoor movie in The Range. We sat under the stars enjoying the breeze and the movie for half an hour. I'd made peace with the fact that we'd have to leave before the end because Toby would need to go to bed, so with that in mind, I enjoyed the experience. Toby was so excited to go to the movies with Mommy.

I never felt afraid there. But I did continue to feel lonely. My need for companionship (and just to be clear: no, I don't mean sex) was strong. I was yearning more and more for a hug, an understanding person who was in my corner. I finally understood what it is to be a single parent. It's an exhausting and lonely task. I thought about my loneliness and the fact that it was self-inflicted. I didn't regret my decision to bring Toby up on my own, but I did regret removing Jacob from Toby's life. As much as I missed having another adult in my life, Toby must have also been missing out on a second adult. I owed it to both Toby and Jacob to arrange for them to meet. I decided then that I would return to Ontario via Red Deer, and make an effort to have Toby meet his father and his grandmother. I owed it to all of them.

The Traveler Card that confirmed that it was time to "Move in a new direction."

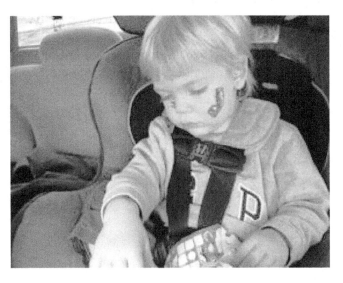

Toby and his stickers on the long drive South.

Toby and his first fishy pet: He touched the eyeballs!

Truck and Trailer at Ancient Oaks

Toby with a couple from Ancient Oaks at Christmas time.

The Head Elf grew his beard every year, and shaved it off again after Christmas.

Me doing the firewalk in Quartzite, Arizona.

Toby and the 'gator in Texas. Look at that big mouth, Mom!

Toby, about to discover that eating olives fresh off the tree is *not* a good idea!

Toby and me at Abu Simbel in Egypt.

Toby and me in front of the Great Pyramid of Giza.

Toby and me on a camel ride in a Bedouin village in Egypt.

Me and my boy in Athens, Greece.

Toby helping to light the gas lamps on the Charles Bridge in Prague.

Christmas in Denmark—with real candles on the tree!

Toby and the Krampus

After swimming through a cave in Thailand, just before my
50th birthday.

Overcoming my fear of heights on my 50th birthday. Some
kind of mid-life crisis?

A typical tourist pose in front of the Taj Mahal.

Toby 'monkeying' around on Elephanta Island with his new 'friend.'

Toby ziplining at Puerto Vallarta

Chapter 8:

Full Circle

In late April 2011, Toby and I were finally back in Peterborough. We moved in with my parents for a month while my tenant finished his year's lease on my house. I thought about the 26,000 kilometers we'd traveled. From freezing winter to balmy ocean shores and back again. The trip back had been hard; it was so cold that despite 'winterizing' the RV, the water in the pipes had frozen.

I had gone back to Red Deer to try and introduce Toby to his dad and grandmother, but was unable to see either of them. I called, and was met with hostility. In fact, I was told to 'fuck off' not only by Jacob, but by his mother too. I persisted, sticking around for a couple of weeks. I did catch up with a few friends during that time, but was quite surprised to find that, despite being there for three Friday nights, I never felt the urge to head to Cheers for karaoke. I was quite content to stay in the trailer with my little man. That would never have been the case in years gone by.

I did eventually manage to arrange to meet Jacob's mother at a coffee shop, and was excited. I didn't tell Toby who we were meeting; firstly, because I wasn't sure how much he'd understand, and secondly, because I didn't want to set him up for disappointment. Once again, my gut instinct did not fail me. I waited for two hours at the coffee shop, and she didn't show up. I gave up then. Their message was clear. They wanted nothing to do with Toby. My heart ached for my child. He deserved so much better, but maybe it was for the best. I certainly didn't want a relationship with Jacob, and maybe Toby would be better off without one too. I eventually gave up and left Red Deer, heading for home.

In Red Deer, I'd finally sold the RV and truck, and bought a little beater car to complete the trip home. Toby and I both bawled like babies as the proud new owners, a young family, drove off in our mobile home. I'd had to be seriously ruthless in deciding what to pack into the car for the homeward journey. For a couple of 'minimalists,' we'd sure collected a lot of stuff on our travels, most of which ended up being temporarily stored in my friend Amanda's garage.

The car had felt so small compared to the truck, and I'd felt even smaller in it, caged. The sense of power and freedom I'd had behind the wheel of the truck was gone. I was insignificant again as we'd crept reluctantly toward our new normal.

"At least the troopers won't stop us," I said to Toby, remembering an incident that had occurred in California. We laughed. We'd been stopped by a couple of state troopers shortly after crossing the state line. They were real 'cool cats,' sauntering up to the vehicle, reflective sunglasses and all. I'd half expected to see the main man chewing on a stem of grass! "Well, well, well, you're not from around here, are ya?" he drawled.

"No, sir," I'd responded. "My plates are Canadian."

"Well, you Canadians come down here and don't really know our laws now, do ya?"

Unable to come up with a polite response, I'd elected to stay silent. I probably didn't know every law in the USA, but wasn't about to admit to anything of the sort.

"So, perhaps you're not aware, little lady, that in the state of California, you require a special driver's license to pull a trailer. A big trailer like yours... Now, how long is your trailer?"

"Twenty-seven feet."

"Well now, we have a problem. You see, in California, you need a special license to pull anything over twenty-five feet. I'm going to need your license and registration."

I'd handed over my Class One driver's license, which qualified me to drive a 53-foot trailer. He'd swaggered back to his vehicle with my papers. It felt like at least 15 minutes had passed before he returned.

"Now, now, this is a Class One license."

"Yes, sir." I'd responded with my sweetest smile. "Is that not a high enough class of license to be able to tow a little 27-foot trailer in the fine state of California?"

The officer handed me my license and registration and, in a curt tone said, "Have a nice day, ma'am."

I'd driven off feeling six feet tall! When I was a young child, we'd lived near a six-lane divided highway overpass, and I'd often walked to the overpass to watch the trucks roll by and dream of one day being behind the wheel of one of those majestic large vehicles. I'd even asked for an 18-wheeler for Christmas one year, much to my parents' amusement. They hadn't taken me seriously, but I'd insisted. I still have that toy truck, and it's provided Toby with as many hours of delight as it did me.

I also thought of our visit to Area 51, where my friend Eric had met up with us for a couple of days on our return journey. I'd wanted to visit him on our trip, but it was just too far out of the way, and he'd compromised by meeting us en route for a few days. It had been fun talking rubbish about aliens and life in general. I was going to miss footloose traveling days. Judging by the number of times that Toby referred back to the trip, so was he. We'd both felt quite bereft at the end of the journey.

At this stage of our lives, I was feeling like a lamb to the slaughter. Life was a journey, and the next leg of the journey felt all wrong to me. I didn't look forward to it. I spent a lot of time reflecting. It was hard to believe that six months had passed so quickly, and as some of the memories of the trip faded, it sometimes felt like it had just been a dream. I thought about all the things we saw, and wondered what we'd missed when we rushed. We'd spent weeks in the desert living as minimalists and flower children. Had it made my heart sing? Yes, and no. I'd learned some valuable life lessons; we'd certainly bonded in a way that we may not have achieved in an 'ordinary' world. But, other than a somewhat different 'holiday,' what had I accomplished?

Had I 'found' myself? Not really. I'd gotten to know myself and Toby better, but I hadn't grown spiritually; I hadn't reconciled my own duality. Even as I'd packed, stressed, prepared to return to working life, and played two-year-old's games, I'd mentally started planning our next big adventure. This return to routine was a means to an end. I knew in my heart that it was more about financial recovery rather than carving out a future career. There was still something missing from my life.

Toby and I soon settled into a very humdrum existence of day care and work. One thing about condominium management, it doesn't keep office hours. I was on call 24 hours a day, seven days a week. It was both exhausting and stressful. I began to have some understanding of how my mother must have felt during her career. I'd resented her work, feeling that it was more important to her than her children. Now that I was in her shoes, I was torn by guilt. When I was working, I felt guilty about neglecting Toby. When I was spending time with Toby, I felt guilty about neglecting my work. There was precious little time to spend on personal relationships.

Then I met Chris, a contractor who had been doing a job at one of the properties I was managing. I don't know if we fell in love, or if I was just desperate for companionship. But it was a very intense relationship. We spent every spare moment together. Like Kevin, Chris was paying child support to his ex for three daughters. The relationship was very short-lived; six months to be exact. He lived at home with his mother and bad-mouthed his exes. Why had I not learned? Men who live with their parents and have nothing good to say about their exes should have warning labels.

It didn't take long for me to realize that he was hiding something from me. Despite the intensity of the relationship, I only met his daughters once. We contrived to 'bump into' each other in the park one day, and I was introduced as a colleague from work. He said that he didn't want to introduce me officially until he was sure that this was a long-term relationship. I understood the logic of that, though I didn't apply the same logic to his meeting Toby. Toby was younger, and I didn't think he'd be concerned about where and how Chris fit into our lives.

I felt a bit of a sense of déjà vu when I ended up with the bill after dinners out, but couldn't really blame him. After all, he had all that child support to pay. I felt sure that something was not right, though. I sensed that he had a lot of secrets. This was confirmed when I spoke to him about my ability to see and sense things; he immediately started pulling back, as though he was afraid of what I might find out about him.

I was worried about what he might be hiding, and started questioning my relationship. Eventually, one Saturday, I decided to have a reading with a psychic and see what came up in terms of relationships. "There is a man who you need to be wary of. A man with three daughters. He is not good for you in any way." I was quite shaken by this. I hadn't told the psychic that I was seeing a man with three daughters, and she didn't know me, or Chris. That was enough to frighten me off, and I immediately broke things off with Chris. I never saw him again.

One night, Kevin called out of the blue, in a very sorry state. His voice was slurred and he was an emotional wreck. Everything in his life was wrong. We talked for a while, me trying to coax him into a positive frame of mind, and him countering each argument with more negativity. Eventually, frazzled, I said, "Kevin. I can't do this anymore. Booze is your biggest problem! Clean up your act and sort yourself out. Until then, please, lose my phone number." I put the phone down with mixed feelings. Kevin had played a big part in mine and Toby's lives; he'd been the one to encourage us to take our journey, and live our truth. I felt like I was letting him down by not sticking by him through his depression. At the same time, though, I thought he needed a wake up call. He had so much potential when he was sober. I felt a bit like the pot calling the kettle black, given my past relationship with alcohol, but I'd seen the damage it could do, and knew that until he could face that reality, there was nothing more I could do for him.

One morning, only 14 short months after our return to "normalcy", while heading out to one of the condominiums, my mobile rang.

"Hello, Marnie speaking," I answered.

"Marnie, hi, it's Fred."

"Oh, hi Fred." He was my boss. "How are things?"

"Actually, not all that good." He paused.

"How so?"

"You know the new American crew that bought out the company?"

"Yeah."

"Well, they're closing all the offices outside of the greater Toronto area."

I was stunned. "What does that mean for us?"

"Well, it means you're out of work."

"Oh shit! When?"

"As of now."

Just like that, I was out of a job. I continued on my way to the condominium and completed my day's work mechanically, numb.

That night, I railed at the universe. How could life be so unfair! How could I have given up my dreams for this job only to have it taken away so soon? What was the point?

Over the next few days, the point became clear. The closure of the office meant that clients were left without management. I was approached by the board of the largest contract to start my own company and take them on as a client. I was excited by the idea, but nervous too. I hadn't thought of striking out on my own, and there was the not insignificant non-competition clause in my contract. Together with the board, I approached the company in Toronto and asked to be released from the non-competition clause, seeing as it was them walking away. They agreed. McBain Property Management was born.

For the first time, I felt really motivated. I was doing something on my own, for myself. I wasn't just a worker; I was creating something. I only had one client, but I worked hard at proving that I was worthy of their trust. I could do this. I threw myself into work, and four months later, I picked up a second client. My parents were proud of me. Hell, I was proud of me!

Toby was not so proud of me. He needed more attention and had no understanding of what it meant to run a company (albeit a small one). To make up for the guilt of working all hours of the day and night, I tried to spend as much time with Toby as I could. The end result was that there was no time for Marnie. If I wasn't working, I was parenting. It felt like I was on a treadmill, but a heady one at that. I was superwoman, taking on the world and single parenting at the same time.

Until I got sick. Toby and I had gone away for a rare weekend to my parents' cottage at the lake. We had spent a wonderful evening eating bread and honey while lying on the dock, watching the mist rising from the lake in the light of an almost full moon. The following morning, we'd joined up with a couple of other families for a lovely day boating on the lake. Toby and I skimmed the water in a tube towed by the boat, giggling and hanging on for dear life, until the tube bumped across the wake and tossed us into the water. I got a noseful, but didn't give it any further thought, until later that day when I was struggling with my sinuses. In the late afternoon, I started sneezing, my nose itched, I developed a rash, my ears were sore, and my eyes were red and watering.

I had never suffered from allergies, but my brother and father always did at a certain time of the year, so I dug out some antihistamine pills from the cottage's bathroom cabinet, and took those. It turned out that I was reacting to the pesticides and herbicides that leached into the lake from surrounding farmlands. This was exacerbated by the water warming up and the algae beginning to bloom. I took the antihistamines for a few days after the weekend, as some of the symptoms persisted.

Around this time, I was at work when it felt as though my arm and face were numb. I rubbed at my arm with the other hand; it felt dead. This was followed by a woozy feeling. I staggered dizzily to a chair and plonked myself down.

"Marnie! Marnie! Are you okay? Speak to me!" I opened my eyes to see one of my colleagues leaning over me, looking concerned.

"Don't know… I feel weird. Sort of car sick, dizzy. Like vertigo." My voice sounded thick and far away.

"Come on, Marnie. Stand up. Here. I'll help you; we need to get you to the hospital." She put an arm around me and hauled me to my feet.

Just walking was hard work; my body was exhausted and not very cooperative. I spent the whole day at the hospital, having one test after another. They were puzzled. It appeared that I had had a Transient ischemic attack (TIA); in layman's terms, a temporary blockage of an artery or mini-stroke. Fortunately, the doctor said it wouldn't have any long term effects, but he told me that my body was sending me a serious warning. I needed to slow down, or risk a full blown stroke. Within hours, I felt better, and was home by late afternoon.

I did try to slow down, and to spend more time with Toby. He was now only three years old, and would still need me for many more years to come. Blood tests went on for some time, as the doctor tried to work out what had caused the TIA. Eventually, he put it down to a bad reaction to the antihistamines I'd taken. I was annoyed with mankind for messing with nature with all those chemicals that had gotten into the lake. It always came back to man. If it hadn't been for man's interference, I'd never had to take that antihistamine in the first place. I now had to avoid swimming in the lake at certain times of the year.

What I couldn't do, though, was slow down completely. I was now responsible not only for myself and Toby, but my clients and employees too. My little business was growing, and needed just as much attention as Toby did. I decided that it was time to make time for another person in my life. I needed someone to share my load, or at the very least, to provide me with some moral support. I'd been alone for too long.

I, very hesitantly, looked at Internet dating sites. That would be easier than leaving Toby with babysitters while I went and hung out at bars or clubs hoping to meet other singles. Besides which, bars and clubs lose quite a lot of their appeal when you become an occasional drinker.

I met a man on the Internet; let's call him, Steve (I'm not all that keen on being sued!). Initially, our email chats were quite superficial. Finding out about each other, where we grew up, and what foods and music we enjoyed. After a week or two, the conversations became a bit deeper; we discussed broader issues that irritated us, or what made us happy. I told him about my travels and the rainbow people. He said that he liked the fact that I was a free spirit, and he didn't seem in the least bit perturbed by my psychic side.

So, when he suggested just before the weekend that we meet and go out to celebrate Valentine's day on Saturday, my heart did a little happy dance. I agreed, and he responded by sending the details. He was inviting me to a swinger's party! He said he couldn't go alone, as no single males were allowed, so even if I was not into 'that,' maybe I could still go, so he'd be allowed in!

Where the hell was my sixth sense during my email discussions with him? Did technology interfere with it?

I responded by email as usual:

Dear Steve,

Thank you so much for the invitation to take you to a swinger's party on Saturday night. I'm flattered that you think so much of me that you'd like to see me naked on our first date. I was always under the impression that swingers are usually partners prior to these events, and as such, are able to brag about their partner's sexual prowess in order to lure some new partners into the fray. So now I have to ask, have you talked to any of my ex's who've told you how amazing I am in bed? Because then you can honestly (and your profile says you never lie) tell potential partners at the party how my blow jobs blow your mind! Maybe you are missing the sarcasm in this message. So, let me be more direct. I'm not stuck up, I don't have my head in the sand, and who knows, maybe one day I would swing with my partner... BUT, you are not my partner. I've never met you in person, and until a couple has a solid foundation of trust, love, kindness, and many other things, they should not be looking to have their partner sleep with them and others on a first date!

Sorry, I'm out.

Marnie

I decided that Internet dating was not for me. I was better off meeting people in person and being able to get a feel for them. There was also no rush. I would continue to manage on my own.

About a year after I'd last spoken to Kevin, I had a problem with my laptop. I needed it fixed in a hurry. So, as Kevin had been my go-to guy for anything vaguely technological, and he was in the IT business, I decided to give him a call.

"Could you look at my laptop for me?" I asked. "It's giving trouble."

Kevin sighed. "I can. You can drop it off at my place, but Marnie, I've made some big changes in my life. I've given up drinking, and I don't want to get sucked back into that lifestyle, so I don't want to see people that I associate with my drinking days. That includes you. So put the laptop on my step, ring the doorbell, and leave. I'll call you when it's fixed and arrange to get it back to you."

I was happy for Kevin that he'd kicked alcohol. I felt sure that this would be the making of him. I knew it was wrong, but suddenly, I wanted to see him. I wanted to tell him that I was proud of him. So, I cheated. I parked a distance from his home and walked to the door with my laptop. I rang the doorbell, and waited quietly. After about five minutes, the door opened. He looked better than when I'd last seen him—no surprises there, seeing as he'd been drunk then.

The look of shock on his face when our eyes met flooded me with guilt. "Sorry, Kevin. I know you didn't want to see me. But I just had to see you and tell you that I'm proud of you. You're doing a great thing, for yourself and your girls."

"Thanks, Marnie. Your blunt talk was what got to me. But it's only been a year, and I'm scared of relapsing. So, I think you need to go."

"I will," I said, stepping back from the door as he took the laptop from me. "It's just. Well, I wanted you to know."

He turned and went inside, closing the door behind him. I stood in front of the closed door for a moment, then walked back to my car. I felt happy on my drive home. Happy that Kevin had sobered up, happy that I had my own business, and happy that I was Toby's mom. Toby's behavior was still a bit erratic. I'd hoped that when he turned three, the terrible twos would have come to an end, but no such luck. The tantrums and bad behavior were less frequent, though, and the adorable moments in between, when he giggled as I tickled him until he yelled, "Enough! Enough!" or when he crept up to me and begged for kisses, more than made up for the tough times.

Yes, I was still stretched thin, and on one occasion, when I'd had a bout of food poisoning and was desperate for time alone in the bathroom, I'd wished there was someone else to take over 'duties.' He'd come into the bathroom while I was throwing up, saying, "Mommy, Mommy, when are you going to come and play?"

"I'm sick, Toby."

"I'm sick too, Mommy. Come and play. Come, Mommy, Mommy, please Mommy!"

I'd eventually placated him with an afternoon on the couch in front of the television. I was learning that sometimes it was okay to not be hands on all the time. Sometimes, a bit of electronic distraction can actually be good for both parent and child. I later discovered that a number of my friends (who had a spouse or partner at home) also did this from time to time. It wasn't the end of the world and didn't cause any harm. It didn't make me a bad parent.

When my computer was ready, Kevin called me to say I could come and fetch it. This time, he let me in when I rang the doorbell.

"Come in. I want to ask you something."

I went inside and he offered me a soda. I was curious.

"Marnie. This has been a hard road for me to walk alone. I cut myself off from all of my friends, and I'm lonely."

I nodded, understanding that kind of loneliness.

"So… I want to ask if I could take you and Toby out for a meal once a month? My treat."

"Ah. Kevin. I'm not sure…"

"It wouldn't be a 'date' as such, Marnie. I'm not looking for a romantic relationship. I understand we're finished. I just…I just need a friend who I can hang out with, who understands my issues and is willing to support me. I think you could be that person."

"Okay, yes, I think I could be. Toby would love to see you. Okay. Let's give it a try, see how it goes."

"Thank you, Marnie. It means a lot." His smile reached his eyes for the first time. I was glad I hadn't said no.

The first date-that-wasn't-a-date, took place a couple of weeks later. We went out for sushi. Toby pulled out all the stops. He ran around the restaurant, yelling and skidding into other diners' tables. When I tried to catch him and calm him down, he yelled even louder. Conversation was almost impossible. I was distracted and embarrassed, and Toby was hell on wheels.

Kevin tried to leave halfway through dinner. I didn't want him to. He was paying for the meal, and we were ruining it. I felt I should leave. In the end, we both stuck it out politely.

It was a relief when the meal was over and I could get Toby home, where he instantly relaxed and smiled sweetly as I put him to bed, looking like butter wouldn't melt in his mouth. I wasn't falling for his manipulative charm and left him to go to sleep on his own. I was pretty sure that would be the last I'd see of Kevin.

I was surprised when he called me again a month later and asked if he could take Toby and me to dinner again. I laughed. "You're a sucker for punishment!"

"No." He laughed too. "Just need some company."

"Okay," I said. "I just can't guarantee the quality of it."

"No problem. Let's try, though. I've got to get out of these four walls."

"Alright, but it's at your own risk!"

The second 'non-date' went better. Toby was calm, and we enjoyed the outing. It soon became a monthly routine, which went on for about a year.

In January 2014, Kevin called to arrange our regular month end dinner. "Sorry, I can't," I said guiltily. "I've got plans."

"Oh?" He didn't sound upset. Just curious.

"Yeah. It's my birthday, and I've got a babysitter for Toby. I've put an open invitation on Facebook for my friends to meet me at the bar for a karaoke evening."

"Of course. Shit! Sorry, Marnie. I'd forgotten. Happy birthday!"

"No problem. I don't expect you to remember."

"Yeah, but still… I'll tell you what. Why don't I come and hang out with you for a bit at the bar? Keep you company until your friends show up?"

"I… Are you sure?"

"Yeah. I won't drink, and I'll leave when your friends arrive, but I think I'm ready to give it a try. I can't spend the rest of my life locked up."

"Okay! Great. I won't let you drink! That'll be nice. Thanks, Kev… Are you sure you're sure?"

He laughed. "It's your birthday and I'm sure. It'll be nice. I can do this."

My Facebook invitation had been for seven p.m., so I arranged to meet Kevin at six. That way, he wouldn't have to leave as soon as he arrived. I made a special effort with my appearance. Going out in the evening, without Toby, felt naughty and grown up. I was excited and looking forward to a whole evening of adult conversation, and some fun. Who knew, maybe I'd meet someone. Toby was staying over with the babysitter, so I had no curfew. I played music in my room as I made up my face, and even smiled at my reflection in the mirror.

Kevin arrived punctually at six o'clock, and we each ordered a soda. I felt like having a whiskey, but decided that could wait. I'd feel guilty drinking in front of Kevin. At quarter past seven, I looked at my watch then glanced around the room. None of my friends had arrived yet.

"Can I get you another soda?" Kevin asked.

"No. Don't worry. I'm sure they'll be here soon. You don't have to hang around if you want to get home."

"Don't be silly. I'm not going to leave you here on your own." He walked over to the bar and came back carrying two Shirley Temple's.

"Here. Cheers to your birthday." He clinked glasses with me, and I smiled at him. He was doing so well.

By eight o'clock, Kevin was still there keeping me solitary company. My anticipation of a fun night out had dampened.

None of my friends had arrived. Without even one whiskey, I was on a downward slide to a pity party.

"Hey, don't worry. They're probably just running late. Who are you expecting?"

"I don't know. Nobody, by the looks of things." I blinked back threatening tears. "I didn't send out individual invitations. I just put it on Facebook. I didn't expect hordes of people, but I did think someone might actually want to celebrate with me."

"It's still early."

"No. It's not, Kevin. It's an hour late." The first tear slid down my face. "This isn't the first time this has happened. When I was at school, I once invited friends to a birthday party at my house and nobody showed up. What's wrong with me?"

"Hey. There's nothing wrong with you, and I showed up. Didn't I? Come on. Cheer up. I'll be back in a sec." He stood and walked over to the bar counter.

He handed me a glass on his return, and I put it to my lips. Whiskey. A double, judging by the taste. "Ah, Kevin…"

"It's okay, mine's a Shirley Temple." He grinned. "I'm big. I can take it."

So began a long evening as I drank one whiskey after another. Drowning my sorrows. Kevin was true to his word and stayed sober, while I worked on earning my first hangover in years.

The next morning was like a scene out of *Groundhog Day* when I woke to a sleeping Kevin, this time in *my* bed.

Chapter 9:

Change Isn't Always for the

Better

When I'd first woken up, I'd been angry. Angry with Kevin, and angry with myself. I had been so in control of my drinking, and the previous night, in my emotional state, I had lost that control. This was the second time that alcohol had shifted our relationship from platonic to physical. I stewed for a while, then in a moment of honesty, had to admit that while I'd shucked all inhibition due to the booze, I remembered the evening with surprising clarity. I had to recognize my own role in this shift. I could have stopped it. I didn't. I had been under the influence of alcohol, not Kevin. He'd stayed to make sure that I got home safely. Maybe it was a case of in vino veritas again?

Maybe I needed Kevin in my life. I was embarrassed. Kevin wasn't. He took it in his stride, and simply accepted that we were now a couple again. I didn't take too much convincing to come to the same level of acceptance. It was nice to have my own person. Someone with whom to share burdens, plan and hope with. It wasn't long before Kevin moved back in with

Toby and me. We became a family, and it was a relief not to be the only person trying to hold things together.

Probably because we had lived together previously, Toby didn't turn a hair. It was as if Kevin had just been waiting for us to get back from our 'holiday' and things were back to normal. In the first year or so, if people referred to Kevin as Toby's dad, Toby would be quick to correct them. "Kevin's not my dad; he's my mom's boyfriend." But after a while, I noticed that he stopped doing it. He just let the error pass.

Toby was five when this all happened. He was more aware of what was happening around him and starting to understand relationships, and give and take—though this was still more skewed in favor of take than give. Now when he played with other kids at kindergarten, he actually played *with* them, not just alongside them. It wasn't just about sharing toys; it was about talking and interacting. I loved this stage of his life. He was still up for a cuddle, a tickle, and a kiss, but he was showing signs of independence. He wanted to decide what to wear, and was developing his own likes and dislikes. It was fascinating to be able to talk to him and hear his opinions on things.

Kevin was good with Toby, and they developed a bond. Later that year, Kevin and I both got our motorcycle licenses and bought motorbikes. I was able to pay cash for mine. I had an issue with taking loans to buy things. Other than a mortgage, and sometimes a car loan, I preferred to wait until I could afford something instead of satisfying my wants by putting myself into debt. Even on the occasions in my life that I had taken a loan to pay for a car, I'd paid it off as quickly as possible and then driven it payment free for a few years.

When we hit the road on our bikes, Toby would usually elect to ride with Kevin. Mostly I suspect because Kevin's bike was big and had a deep thunderous roar. More macho. Despite the fact that I'd always been a bit of a dual soul in terms of femininity and machismo—switching between wearing butterfly dresses and driving trucks—it was clear that there were benefits for Toby in having a male influence in his life, and now that the male influence was sober, even more so. I felt almost sorry for his biological dad, Jacob, that he was missing out on being that inspiration. I think he had more than enough children to influence, though—rumour had it that Jacob now had four children. One with me, two with Sarah, and another one with some other poor girl, born within months of his and Sarah's second (though he was denying paternity in that case). I also heard via the grapevine that he and Sarah were no longer together. I had to remind myself that not every male influence is a good one.

That September, when Toby turned six, I bought us both bicycles. His balance was good, and it wasn't long before we were taking rides together. We both looked forward to these. While it meant we were separate, unlike on the motorbikes where he was always a passenger, it was quieter, and gave us more opportunity to connect and chat as we cycled, mostly on quiet country lanes. Toby shared my enthusiasm for nature.

I was still working hard, but somehow, with three of us at home, we'd found a sense of balance. I continued to suffer twinges of guilt over balancing parenting and work, but they were less agonising, and felt less dire. I was getting more out of both roles. I'd taken on new clients in my business and was hosting seminars that people traveled far to attend. I was also finding time to spend doing kid stuff. Thank goodness the level of kid stuff had expanded, making it more enjoyable for both of us! Toby and I worked in my vegetable patch, loving watching things grow, and gaining huge satisfaction from preparing and eating our own produce.

We still drew and painted. One weekend, we spent nearly a whole day on our hands and knees in the driveway decorating it with colored chalk. We drew flowers, the sun, clouds, and mountains, and wrote, "Save the planet," "Be kind to the earth," Gandhi's famous quote, "Be the change you wish to see in this world," and Etta Turner's, "In a world where you can be anything, be yourself." If our neighbors had suspected me of being a bit of a hippie before, this probably confirmed it for them.

I even made time to explore my intuition and look for a deeper, more spiritual meaning to life. I did course after course on improving my awareness. I felt that I was more 'awake' to reality than I'd ever been. I needed to understand what was 'real.' Mankind would have you think that being responsible, having a job, gathering wealth, and avoiding being scammed is 'reality.' I couldn't just accept that. Is that what we're born for? To survive the rat race and accumulate wealth? Is life all about technology, development, and advancement? Surely not. When I see the damage made to the world in the name of 'development,' I shudder and wonder if we're not getting things horribly wrong.

Despite all of the material successes I was experiencing, I still felt that I had not found my true path in life. That I was living a lie. I gave up alcohol altogether. I couldn't think of a time that it's 'benefits' had ever outweighed the harm that it caused. I started to appeal to psychics and intuitive counsellors to help me find my way. The more I did this, the more interested I became in the meaning of life, and finding one's own truth. I studied. I did more courses than I could count. I had previously qualified as a Reiki Master, a Past Life Regressionist, and a Certified Hypnotherapist, but this didn't feel like enough. I wanted more. I wanted to understand how people fit into the universe, how they impact each other and their environments. Mostly, I wanted to know how to know, really *know*, that what they are thinking and doing is right. To be in touch with that 'gut feeling,' recognize it, and use it to achieve more. By 'more' I don't mean more material things; I mean more personal fulfilment. I began to wonder if doing this for others was my true calling.

I even started reading about mediums, and how they connect with the spirit world. All of this drove the wedge between me and my brother deeper. The more clarity I gained, the more he thought I was going off the rails. He didn't believe in 'bullshit.' Our belief systems were growing further and further apart, making family gatherings more and more tense. I have great sympathy for my parents during this period of our lives, as they tried to keep the peace and encourage family unity while also struggling to understand my spiritual development, and accept my forays into the non-physical realm of existence.

I understood and accepted that not everyone is comfortable 'going there,' and many choose to view life in a more superficial and pragmatic manner. I even understood *why*.

Exploring thoughts, feelings, and connections can be hard work; it can also be painful. It's easier to close the closet door on all that and deal with life on a less connected level. BUT, I couldn't understand why, if you *are* connected, if you *are* intuitive and *have* visions, you should be expected to hide that from the world, to be ashamed of it. To me, it was a gift to be nurtured. I didn't ask to be the way I was, but I wasn't ashamed of it. I was fascinated.

Same sex marriages had been legalised in Canada about ten years prior. It was a time when the world was coming around to the notion of choosing your own gender or electing to be transgender. People recognized that those who didn't conform to being simply male or female and sexually 'straight' didn't choose to be that way, nor were they 'sick.' Anyone who didn't agree was labelled a bigot. I couldn't understand why it was okay to identify as a different gender, and even change genders, but not to be psychic. I couldn't see the shame in it. I still can't.

While I was wrestling with these deep thoughts, Toby was wrestling with issues of his own. I noticed that his enthusiasm for school had decreased, but thought it was just a passing phase. However, when he started resisting going to school, my radar was up. Skeptics of course would say, but I thought you were psychic? How come you didn't know what was worrying him? Can't you read minds? The answer is complicated, but the simple version is no. 'Mind reading' is more of a parlor trick than anything else. Psychics 'read' and recognize emotions, and ideas, not words. Visions come to them, sometimes randomly and sometimes through focus on the issue at hand, as does intuition, but it's not a case of seeing every thought inside every person's head at all times. My focus at that time was very diverse. I was focusing on my business, my relationship with Kevin, and my studies. Of course, I was focusing on Toby too, but more on entertaining and educating him than anything else. I had never sat down and done a reading for him.

Something was clearly wrong at school. I asked him about it, and he said, "I don't know. I just don't like school anymore." I sat quietly, waiting for him to speak again. "Okay, so there's one boy who is mean. I don't like him."

"What does he do that's mean?"

"He pushes me and breaks things, and he says mean stuff."

"Try and stay away from him then, but don't let him ruin your day, or take away your happiness. If you have any problems, you must report it to the teacher, okay?"

He nodded. "Okay." But I sensed that it was not okay. He wasn't the kind of child who liked ratting others out. I hoped that avoiding this child would help. A few days later, Toby was pushed down the stairs, and tumbled into students walking ahead of him. He came home bruised. I was furious and made an appointment to see the school principal. That didn't go well. It started with the principal saying that Toby had hurt a few children, knocking them down the stairs, and that he should be considered for suspension. Toby's little face was white, and I didn't even need to see him shake his head to know that he was flabbergasted. I exploded. Eventually, after I'd calmed down, Toby had been allowed to tell his side of the story.

These incidents continued over a period of four months, with Toby being physically injured five times. I was a regular visitor at the school, and the principal, on the occasions that she couldn't avoid me, always looked pained to see me.

The last time, Toby came home from school one day in a mess. He was covered in mud from head to toe. His new winter jacket was destroyed, one sleeve completely torn. His eyes were red and swollen from crying.

"Oh no! Toby, what happened?" I could feel his anguish.

"One of the big boys pushed me in the mud at recess, and he pulled me and rolled me in the mud."

"Didn't you tell the teacher?"

Toby shook his head, a tear sliding down the mud caked on his cheek. I was incensed. I called the school and spoke to the principal.

"Why didn't the school call me?"

"Mrs. McBain." I could hear the exaggerated patience in the principal's voice. "If the teacher had noticed that Toby was covered in mud in class, she would have reported the matter. The matter was not reported." I could hear the doubt in her voice.

"I'm not making this up. Toby is standing in front of me, covered in mud, and his jacket is ruined. His face is swollen from crying. How can the teacher not notice that?"

"I understand. I'm not calling him a liar..."

The hell you're not, I thought.

"Tomorrow I'll personally take Toby from class to class and he can identify the person that did it, okay?"

"No! That's not okay. How can you even suggest making a young child identify his attacker in person? Has he not been through enough? Toby said Miss Phipson separated the kids on the playground herself. Ask her to identify the bully, and while you're about it, ask her what kind of an Educators Assistant she is to not have reported the issue or enforced any discipline."

Toby did return to school, but the seed had been planted in my mind. I started looking into different home schooling options. I knew what it felt like to be bullied at school; it had crushed me, and I wanted to spare Toby that pain. Things needed to change. Little did I know that all my plans would be put on hold shortly thereafter.

It was labor Day Monday, 2015, the last day of summer vacation before school went back. Toby and I decided to jump on our bicycles and ride down the hill to get ice cream. Kevin offered to take his truck down and meet us at the shop, so that we could load our bicycles on the back for the return, saving us the steep ride home. We were excited.

I headed out in front with Toby hot on my tail. As I turned the corner at the bottom of our street, I heard Toby call out. I turned my head. He'd fallen off his bike on the turn; he was uninjured and was busy climbing back on, yelling, "Wait up, Mom!"

There was a school bus stop about 20 meters ahead, and I was busy turning my head back to the front, gently applying the breaks, yelling back to Toby, "I'll wait at the bus stop!"

The next thing I remember, I was lying on the road with Toby leaning over me, his face a picture of concern, saying, "Get up, get up, Mommy!"

I tried to move and excruciating pain from my shoulder stopped me.

"Come on, Mommy. Before a car comes. We need to go to the driveway."

I struggled to lift myself from the tarmac, leaning heavily on Toby. "No. The grass, Toby. Get me to the grass." My legs were jellylike and uncoordinated, but working. My entire upper body was engulfed in searing pain. I couldn't work out where one pain ended and the next began. I collapsed on the grass bank to the merciful relief of oblivion.

My next memory was of Toby on his knees at my side, sobbing. I heard Kevin's voice, fuzzy in the distance. "Yes, ambulance...to the corner of Whitefield and Afton...no there's no fuckin' address; you can't miss us...it's urgent...she's hurt bad, yes bicycle...no, no address, you don't need an address just get here, to the corner!" He ran to my side after getting off the phone. "Hang in there, hun, an ambulance is coming."

I tried to tell him to quit the dramatics and pop my shoulder back in place, but the words kept coming out slurred and wrong. My voice sounded thin and blurred. The pain was intense. Kevin leaned in closer as I tried to repeat my message. Oh God. My shoulder was killing me. I was sure it was dislocated. "Hun," I tried for a third time, "Push my shoulder back."

He shook his head. "Marnie. You're hurt—real bad. I can't fix this one for you, babe. Just stay with us."

I dragged my right hand to my left shoulder. Shit! The collar bone was broken. I tried to tell Kevin. But he just shook his head again. "I can't hear you, babe. Don't try to talk. Just lie still." His face was tense and white. He had one arm around Toby.

I gave up and let the darkness envelope me again.

When I came to again, bright lights reflecting off white tiles hurt my eyes. My head throbbed dully, as did everything else. I was in a hospital bed, with a drip attached. It took me a while to work out what I was doing there. My parents, Kevin, and Toby were at my bedside, with a doctor.

"Marnie, can you hear me?" the doctor asked. I flinched as I tried to nod; my neck was held still by a padded brace. Every little movement hurt.

"You've had an accident. Your neck is broken at C7 and you have two more vertebrae in your cervical spine that are fractured. There are also serious fractures at T3 and T5. Your right shoulder is dislocated and severely separated. You've broken 3 ribs, and your left lung is punctured. The puncturing has collapsed the lung. That's why you're having difficulty breathing. There is also some bleeding into your chest cavity. You're in the ICU ward; you couldn't ask for better care. So just relax and focus on healing, okay?"

I couldn't nod or speak, so I just blinked. Then I let my eyes close again. I was so tired. I heard the doctor addressing my father.

"Mr. McBain, your daughter has a serious concussion. The CAT scan indicates bleeding on the brain. It's very important that we get that stopped. If we can't, we'll have to airlift her to Toronto or Kingston where they have better equipped trauma facilities."

"No!" It was Toby's voice. I wished I could reach out and hold him, but my body was too sore, and my brain too fuzzy to respond.

Over the next three days, I slipped in and out of consciousness. I remember sipping on water, then puking. The pain of my body tensing to throw up was awful. I also remember fending off a nurse who wanted to insert a catheter, using a bedpan, and throwing up from the exertion. I was a mess.

They did manage to get the brain bleed to stop, and I was eventually moved to a general ward. My parents were incredible, helping with Toby and making the 45-minute drive to visit me. Kevin visited every day. On one of these visits, he gave me more information on what had happened.

"I was driving down the hill when I saw Toby running right up the middle of the street. I thought, damn we've got to teach him to walk on the sidewalk, he's going to get run over! When I stopped, he pulled the driver's door open. It was only then that I realized you weren't with him. I said 'what's wrong?' and he just said, 'Mommy' and burst into tears. I said, 'where's your mom?' but the little guy just fell to his knees crying so hard he couldn't talk. I grabbed him and shoved him into the truck, and took off down the hill without even closing the door. As I came around the corner, your bike was still in the road. I pulled up behind your bike, and jumped out, leaving the truck there. You were on the grass next to the road.

"After I called the ambulance, a woman came out of the house nearby and started screaming at me. I s'pose with the way my truck and your bike were in the road, she thought I'd knocked you off your bike."

I managed a smile. Poor man. Getting blamed when all he was doing was trying to help.

"What did happen?" I asked.

"There was a damaged water main shut off sticking out of the road that had created a pothole. We think your front tire went into that and you were thrown. Geez, Marnie, I got a helluva fright when I saw you. You looked so broken." He swallowed hard. "You were bleeding from your ears and your nose. Not red blood, dark, thick blood. Almost black. I didn't think you were going to live." Then he smiled. "But when the poor ambulance guys started trying to get you out of the fetal position to load you on the backboard, you moaned like a drain. That's when I realized you were still fighting. You won that battle, by the way. And the doctor said it was a good thing you did. He reckons staying curled up might just have saved you from becoming a quadriplegic."

I thought a lot that night about how very fragile and ephemeral life is. You can be here one day and gone the next, without warning or planning. I had written a will when Toby was six months old, thinking at the time that it wouldn't really be necessary for many years to come; it was just a precaution, the responsible thing to do. I was only in my forties. This was a big wake up call.

"They wouldn't let Toby travel with you in the ambulance. So, we followed it in my truck. I phoned my mom, and she met us at the hospital. Thank goodness. Toby was beside himself, and so was I."

Toby filled in more details on his next visit with my parents. "I promise you, Mommy, you somersaulted right off your bike. You bounced. Twice. You get a ten for air acrobatics, but you didn't stick your landing, so you only get three for that. Your bike also bounced on top of you." His face, smeared as it and his T-shirt were with ice cream, shone as he regaled us with his story. I was so glad to see him looking happy again, even if it was at my expense. I still have flashbacks of his little pale face looking into mine with intense concentration, trying to get me to get up and move off the road. I didn't want him to ever have to be alone and without my protection.

"Hey, little monkey. I still can't wait to go and get ice cream with you. You didn't go get any yet, did you?" I teased.

I watched the expression of horror on my little boy's face. I could see him struggling with truth and kindness, and very likely worrying that I'd just know he'd had some. I couldn't leave him hanging.

"Hey, it's okay, monkey. I knew Gramma was taking you for ice cream. I'm only teasing. Come and snuggle carefully next to me."

He clambered onto the bed, and ever so gently lay down next to me. "I'm sorry, Mommy—"

"Don't be a big silly!" I laughed. "It's all my fault. If I hadn't gone and whacked my head off the road, I would have been there for ice cream too."

I was very worried about my business. I was inclined to think I was the only one who could do everything exactly right, so hadn't trained others to handle any of the stuff that I considered 'mine.' So shortly after the move to a general ward, I was taking calls and emails from my hospital bed. It was difficult. The words bounced in front of my eyes. I could barely read. Once I'd made out what the words were, I had to try and get the sentences to make sense. By the time I'd made out the next word, I'd forgotten the gist of what I'd read before. It was frustrating. It was easier if someone read my emails to me. Reports were almost impossible to write.

I started doing more work verbally than in writing, but this too had its drawbacks, because it meant that I didn't have a written record of conversations, and my memory was unreliable. If anyone differed with me, I just had to agree with them because I couldn't back myself up. I was also physically exhausted. I think my body was not only bruised, but traumatised too. Everything I did took so long. This did little to inspire my clients with confidence, and I wasn't surprised when business started to slow.

I was determined not to fail. I even attended a conference in October, in my full neck brace. I ground on doggedly. Toby took up karate lessons at a dojo in Peterborough. Kevin was a black belt in Tae-kwon-do, and one day after picking Toby up from the dojo (school), he suggested that he find another dojo for him. He felt sure that somebody was going to get hurt where he was. He did find another dojo, and after that, Kevin and Toby attended regularly, with Toby switching to Tae-kwon-do and excelling under Kevin's additional tutelage.

I was working longer and longer hours. Not because my business was busy, just because everything was so much slower and harder since the accident. Simple things like reading and writing just took so much longer. My income was also dwindling. Things like Tae-kwon-do lessons were getting beyond my means.

I went and got my bus driver's license and took on a second job, driving the local school bus. This too ate into my time, but I kept pushing myself. I rushed from one job to the next. I look back on those days now and wonder what drove me. Fear of stopping? Fear of lost income? Or the work ethic that had been instilled in me by my parents? Whatever it was, it prevented me from slowing down and giving my body time to heal. I guess in some ways it was good, because I've recently heard that those who engage in cognitive activities immediately after a brain injury have the best outcome. At the time, however, it was insane. I worked all hours, and Toby was lucky to have Kevin to pick up the pieces.

Chapter 10:

From the Impossible to the Possible

For the next three years after the accident, life was a continuous struggle. I was physically and mentally slowed by the injuries to my body and brain. Simple tasks were frustrating and slow to execute. My inability to read and respond to emails was probably one of the worst side effects. These sort of tasks that used to take me minutes to complete were taking hours, and by the time I'd completed them, I was exhausted. I was working at keeping McBain Property Management going, driving the school bus, and in between doing Reiki healing and intuitive counselling.

While Toby has always been my number one priority in life, I was spending less and less time with him as I tried to manage my business and keep income from drying up. So often I've heard people say, "If you fall off the horse, get back on." I was having a hard time doing this practically or metaphorically. I was definitely in no rush to go cycling, but more than that, while I understood that I was lucky to be alive and functioning (albeit slowly), I couldn't put it behind me. I often woke at night in a cold sweat, dreaming of Toby's pale crying face over me as I lay in pain on the grass. Sometimes in those dreams, I left my body and was watching Toby mourn over the body of his mother on the grass. My heart ached for my child, but I couldn't reach him or speak to him; I was floating helpless in the ether.

At times, I wished I had died. I thought that Toby would have been better off financially. But those thoughts didn't last long. Simple things like listening to his stories or him picking a flower for me reminded me that life isn't all about money and things. It's about people and connections. Connections. That was a strange side effect of the accident. I seemed disconnected from everything and everyone around me. Everyone else seemed to be living; I was just existing. Yes, I was busy, but I wasn't engaged. It was a bit how I imagine it would feel if I worked in a factory, with one repetitive job to do, like screwing a lid onto a jar. I would think there comes a time where this physical action takes place without thought.

I was doing that all day, every day. If someone said something funny, I smiled. If I could see they needed sympathy, I offered it. But I didn't feel anything. I didn't feel amused or sympathetic; I was just doing what was expected of me. The only thing I did feel was guilt. Guilt that I was being a fraud. I was an imitation mother, a counterfeit girlfriend, and an impostor at work. I was going through the motions, but nobody was getting any value from me. It was hard to live with myself, never mind others. My mind found the negative in every situation, and even when I forced myself to look for the positive, I couldn't express it. My negativity was starting to grate on others around me. I could see that, but I didn't know how to fix it. I felt numb with helplessness.

Poor Kevin. His life changed just as much as mine. I started expecting him to contribute more to household expenses and chores, and rather than thanking him when he did, I got angry when he didn't. Our sex life suffered too. No, that's an understatement; it didn't suffer. It died. It wasn't that I didn't love or like him anymore; he was still the same person he'd always been. I unfortunately was not. I think that, for men, sex is a physical act, while for women, it is emotional. It's the only reason I can think of for my sudden loss of libido.

If Kevin brushed a hand across my breast, or hugged me for too long, I'd start feeling panicked. I knew he wanted more, and I just didn't have it in me to give it to him. He felt rejected, hurt, and mad, and I felt misunderstood. This was a vicious circle that turned in an ever tightening spiral. It's easy now to look back on it and recognize the issues for what they were. Living in the moment, though, I wasn't as objective. I was angry. Could he not understand that my body and mind weren't ready yet? Did he not get it, that after working for hours a day because of my slowness, that I was exhausted? Why couldn't he see that I owed time to Toby too? I felt helpless, and the future looked very bleak.

For the first year or so after the accident, Kevin did his best to be understanding, but eventually, he just got angry. "Marnie, it's been more than a year," he'd say. "Surely you can't still be too sore or fragile. When are you going to start living again? Or don't you plan to? Ever?"

I was stung by the unfairness of it all. Of course, I wanted to live. In fact, I wanted to travel, to broaden my horizons. I just didn't want to have sex. While I was the handbrake in the bedroom, Kevin was the handbrake when it came to travel. I had done a course on Teaching English as a Foreign Language some years back, and kept suggesting that we could travel and I could teach online. It wouldn't have been difficult for Kevin, as he worked in IT from home; a lot of his work is done remotely anyway. So as fast as I was thinking up excuses to avoid intimacy, he was coming up with his own to avoid leaving home. It had become more and more apparent that he was a homebody and I was a 'gypsy.' He had known this about me from the beginning, and encouraged it, but after I started my own business, I guess he started nurturing the hope that I would settle down. All this while, I'd been yearning to pull up my roots and head out into the world.

None of this had boded well for the future. So, within two years of the accident, it was clear that we were growing apart. I went for therapy; as the change had started with me, it seemed I was the one who was going to have to try and 'change back.' During these therapy sessions, I spoke about my negativity, hopelessness, and detachment. I explained to the therapist that I was numb. Other than anger and negativity, I had few other feelings. She diagnosed me with post-traumatic stress disorder (PTSD).

"Your symptoms are typical of PTSD," she said. "I also think you should do some reading on adrenal fatigue. It's more of a theory at this stage than a medically recognized condition, but it fits with what you are experiencing. There isn't a pill you can take to fix it; it requires a lifestyle change. Meditation, healthy eating, lots of vegetables, taking vitamins, that kind of thing."

"I already do most of those things. I am largely vegetarian. I only eat meat once or twice a week, and I do meditate often." I couldn't get past the unfairness of it all. I'd given up drinking before the accident, I didn't smoke, and I ate heaps of vegetables. "I just don't know what more I can do!"

"Maybe you don't need to do more. Maybe you need to do less?"

"What do you mean?"

"Well. It sounds to me like your diet is not a problem, but maybe your work is? Holding down three jobs would be tough on most people, but on top of PTSD and parenting, I think it might be too much. Would you be able to afford to cut back?"

"No. No way. I get about $400 a month in child support, and although I don't pay rent because I own my own house and the mortgage is low, there are still maintenance costs, utilities, food, car payments, insurance etc."

"Have you registered for the government Child Benefits?"

"Yes, I get another $400 for that. But $800 a month isn't enough to cover Toby's costs, never mind mine."

"Well, give it some thought. Maybe you could move in with family and rent your house out?"

"I already rent out my basement; that brings in another $800 a month. But I think we'd still battle. Not to mention the stress of three generations in one house." I shuddered at the thought, not only for me, but for Toby and my parents. I'd seen other families going to pieces after trying extended communal living. Not to mention, I would lose my financial independence.

"I would suggest a leave of absence from work, but as you work for yourself, that's obviously not an option. Unless you have someone who could take over?"

I shook my head. I'd employed assistants from time to time, but at the time of the accident, I'd been working solo; I had not considered the possibility of being incapacitated for a long period. What a mess.

"Well. I'm not a financial advisor, but maybe you should see one, and explore ways of cutting back on your workload. I strongly recommend that. I think you're heading for burnout, and then you might not have the luxury of deciding for yourself."

This conversation had taken place toward the end of 2017. I didn't go and see a financial advisor, and I didn't give up either of my jobs, but her words stayed in my mind. Every time I was worn out and stressed (which was most days!) I would consider them again. I would tell myself that I had the luxury of deciding my own fate. Just knowing that, somehow, I was in charge, made the helplessness seem less severe, even if I did nothing about it.

About six months later, during yet another argument with Kevin about my withdrawal from those who loved me, he said, "Marnie. You are in control of you. You decide how you want to live and how much effort you want to put into relationships. Nobody else. It seems to me that you just don't want to try!"

This was a wake up call to me. Was I allowing myself to be the victim of circumstances? I started thinking a lot about this. I started focusing more on my options. What did I want to do? That was easy: travel. What was stopping me? Two things: finances, and the fact that Toby, at almost 10 years, old still had at least seven years of schooling to go. There was no way that I'd leave Toby and go off traveling, even if I could afford it. Despite all the issues I was experiencing emotionally, my bond with Toby was stronger, and I couldn't contemplate travel without him.

I thought about my answers. What about Kevin? I cared for Kevin, but our relationship was not in a good space. Over and above my intimacy issues, he'd stopped smoking (or so he'd said). I was all for it, I hated the smell of cigarettes, but what I hated even more was catching him out when he lied about it. I kept finding plastic cigar butts in the garden, and there was nothing wrong with my sense of smell! I pretended to believe him for a while, thinking that he would eventually give up completely, but I was very uncomfortable with the trust issues that this raised. I didn't expect him to give up smoking for me. It was something he wanted to do for himself. So why the dishonesty? Did he feel he was failing me? Why could he not just say, "Yeah, I had one"? It was small in the grand scheme of things, but it eroded the trust in our relationship. I couldn't help wondering if there was anything else he was hiding from me.

The more suspicious I got, the more defensive and angrier he got. There was definitely trouble in paradise. By November of that year, arguments were frequent and intense. After a really bad one, we eventually sat down to discuss it. It was clear that neither of us was happy, and we decided to part ways while we could still salvage a friendship from the relationship.

Two things confirmed our decision for me. One was that Toby was not upset when Kevin moved out of the house. Clearly the tension of the last couple of years had spilled over into his little world, and I regretted that enormously. Despite the fact that we'd tried not to bicker in front of Toby, he was clearly still aware of the discord and, being an empath like me, it had affected him more deeply than I'd realized. The second was a card reading that I'd attended shortly after the break up. I was hoping for insight as to what the future held, but what I got was, "There's a man in your life with three daughters. Be wary. Move forward not backwards." I was stunned. This was the second time I'd been warned about a man with three daughters. The first time, I was sure it referred to Chris. Now I wasn't so certain. Maybe both warnings were about Kevin? Or maybe I should just avoid all men with three daughters going forward? I decided that was probably the safest bet. I had little to no interest in striking up new romantic relationships. Singledom appealed to me, and Toby and our future needed my attention.

Toby continued with his schooling, and I continued with my work, and while there was more peace in the house, Toby continued to battle with incidents of bullying at school, and I was still exhausted. One evening, he and I were watching a movie on television about young teenagers who didn't go to school. Not regular school anyway. They traveled the world with their parents, and learned from experience and discussions rather than straight book learning. "I wish I could have done something like that, Toby," I said after the movie, "but that was never an option when I was at school."

Toby gave me a cheeky grin. "Well, it is now, and I'm still at school…"

"Yeah. But your mom doesn't have pots of money or a rich husband either." I laughed. "Bad luck!"

"Poor me," Toby said, rounding his shoulders and putting on a mock sad face. "Don't worry, Mom, I still love you. I'd rather have you any day than a rich dad."

I was fascinated by the lifestyle and experiences that the teens in the movie had had, and one weekend, I searched Google for more information. I was amazed at how many families were actually doing this. Traveling around the world and educating their kids without formal schooling. The concept even had a name: 'world schooling.' Because reading took so much concentration for me, it took a couple of months before I'd gotten my head around the whole concept. I kept going back to my computer and reading in short spurts.

Toby and I discussed it a lot. It was such an 'out of the box' idea, and so much more exciting than classroom learning. "Anyway," Toby said on one occasion, "the stuff they teach at school is ridiculous. How come they teach things like calculus, but they don't bother with how to fill in a tax return?" I couldn't help but agree. Every child is different, and not all fit into the boxes they should. Their needs and interests differ. But, could a parent actually impart enough knowledge to give a child the right head start in life? It sounded amazing, but also a huge responsibility.

I found a woman online, Lainie Liberti, who had been 'world schooling' her son, Miro, as they traveled the world, for about ten years. They'd started when he was just shy of 10 years old. She had even set up a web page called 'Project World School.' There was a whole community of 'cool' parents, who supported each other both online and in person during their travels, who were living a nomadic lifestyle and giving their children a spectacular, hands on education.

How I'd wished I'd had the money to do something like that. For Toby. And for me.

I was living vicariously through Lainie and Miro's experiences. It got to the point where I felt that I almost knew them, and eventually, I summoned up the courage to reach out to her. I needed to know what it really felt like, to live the dream.

Through her, I learned more; her story really resonated with me. She was a single mom, and had been a successful business woman prior to discovering the world beyond the USA and hitting the road with Miro. She was to become my mentor. She told me that world schooling is about children learning through doing, through experiencing things for themselves. It seemed a really radical concept, but believe it or not, there were some even more radical ones out there! I discovered 'unschooling,' in which the child takes the lead on deciding what and how to learn. It sounded like a very risky thing to do. I couldn't begin to imagine the terrible guilt I'd feel if I were to take Toby out of school, only to find that he ended up with a poor education and no future prospects. I loved the idea of 'world schooling,' though, of traveling with Toby, investigating the history, culture, and geography of different people and areas.

One day, I commented on the website that it would be a dream come true for Toby and me, but that we weren't in a financial position to do it. I was quickly put right. You don't have to have heaps of money to do it. Some families travel more than others, and some in more style than others, but nobody treated it as a vacation. They all lived carefully, stayed in cheap accommodations in lousy neighborhoods, and booked multiple stop flights at unpopular times, like the middle of the night. They lived simply on bread and cheese and vegetable soup and crackers when not sampling street food in the various cities. They took packed lunches with them for full day tours, and refilled bottles of water from taps instead of buying sodas. I was told, "It takes an enormous amount of discipline, no buying souvenirs or luxuries. If you have that kind of discipline, you should be able to manage it on roughly the same amount of money that others spend just living at home. But don't do it if you don't have any savings. You have to have contingency money for when things don't pan out. Also, you have to be committed to making it a learning experience. Plan visits to museums, art galleries, and places of interest. Do lots of homework before each destination, so that you have some knowledge, then learn the rest there."

I was enthralled by the possibilities that this kind of rationale could open for us. I was also terrified at the thought of experimenting with Toby's future. I sat down and did my sums.

With the child support and government child benefits, plus if I rented out the whole house, I'd have a monthly income of roughly $2600. While I wouldn't have to pay for utilities etc., I'd still have to cover things like homeowner's insurance. I eventually figured that the maximum we would have available for our basic needs plus travel would be $2,000 a month. If we planned carefully and combined countries with weaker exchange rates with the more expensive countries, it looked like it was potentially in our reach.

I did have some savings, which we could dip into toward the more expensive flights, and still keep some as a backstop for emergencies. Could I sell my business? I realized then that this was what I wanted most in the world. I wanted to be free to travel and explore the planet with Toby. I needed to get off the treadmill that was my life for my sanity and my health. It became a very scary, but all-consuming passion.

I had been keeping a lot of my research to myself. I hadn't wanted to create an expectation in Toby's mind that I had no chance of fulfilling. Eventually, in February 2019, I was convinced that we could actually do it. It was time to discuss it with Toby and get his opinion.

That was the easy part. Before I'd even finished putting out the proposal, his face was flushed with excitement, and he was having trouble sitting still.

"So, what do you say, little man? Shall we do it?"

"Yes! Yes! Yes! Are you serious?"

"Totally."

"Awesome! I can't wait to tell the kids at school tomorrow!"

My heart did a little skip at this comment. How was he going to cope without company of his own age? I did know from my research that there would be opportunities to meet up with and even stay with other 'world schooling' families during our travels, but this would be now and again. The rest of the time it would just be Toby and me. I thought back to our trip when he'd been a toddler. It had been really hard, and really lonely for both of us in many ways. I had struggled with being the sole lifeline of a toddler, and he'd battled with sharing his 'ownership' of me when we'd met up with others. Things were different, though. At 10, Toby was more companionable, more helpful, and far more independent. He was also curious and could entertain himself if need be. We high-fived, and celebrated with a milkshake and burger that night.

Then came the part where I told my parents. That was not so easy. First, I had to explain exactly what 'world schooling' was, then where I'd gotten this 'cockamamy' idea from. They were still trying to come to terms with my break up with Kevin and were very worried about me being 'on my own.' They'd been married for more than 50 years and didn't understand the concept of enjoying being a singleton.

"What about your business?" my dad asked.

"Well, I'm hoping I can sell it. But if I can't, I'm going to close it."

"You can't, Marnie! You've put so much work into it. How will you cope financially, and what will people think? You've built up a good name for yourself, don't throw it away."

"I don't have a choice. I can't go on the way I am. The migraines, the body pains, and my mental state are making work almost impossible. I'm not spending time with Toby; all I do is work." It was important to me that they understood. "My therapist says I need to take a break. I could either give up working and come and live with you, so that I can live off my rental income, or I can go traveling with Toby. I think this is going to be the better of the two options, and you know I've always wanted to. I am completely burned out. Even working part-time is not going to cut it. I need to take time out to recover. I need a full on RESET. I need to get out of this rut. It's killing me. Besides, I bought a new pack of Oracle cards at the opening of Kawartha Zen Den, and the first time I played with them, I asked if this trip should take place and the traveler card jumped out."

"Cards don't jump, Marnie," my dad said. Maybe I shouldn't have added that last bit. My mom reached out and placed a restraining hand on his arm.

"It's an expression, Dad. You shuffle them and, if one falls out, it's considered a 'jumping card.' Have you ever heard the term 'what falls to the floor comes to the door?'" I could see that this angle was not convincing them. "Okay. Never mind the card. I just know in my heart that this is the right thing for me and Toby. It's something I have to try. If it doesn't work out, I'll come back, but I need to get out of my comfort zone, and I also need to have more time for healing, and for Toby. I've been losing clients because I've been man down with migraines seven or eight days a month. I can't carry on anymore. If I don't sell or close the business, I'll either end up losing it or having a major breakdown. I'm not the person I was before the accident."

"But why didn't you tell us about the migraines?" It was my mom this time.

"I did sometimes."

"I know, but not how bad they were. Or how frequent. Why would you hide that from us?"

"I didn't deliberately 'hide' it from you. But I also couldn't go through life whining forever. There's an old Buddhist saying, 'Pain is inevitable; suffering is optional.' I just didn't want to come across as a suffering victim all the time, and I didn't want to worry you."

"But you might need to have that seen to—"

"I have. I've done everything a good responsible adult should do. I've been to doctors and therapists. It's all related to the accident, and my state of mind, as a result of PTSD and post concussive syndrome. It won't last forever, or at least won't be this bad forever. But right now, I can't carry on."

"But is it wise to travel if you're not well?" my mom asked.

"Well, the pain prevents me from concentrating too hard, but Mom, think about it. The alternative is to stay home and have no outside stimulation. I am already in a really bad place mentally. That'll only make it worse. If I'm stuck licking my wounds and feeling sorry for myself, I'll never get better."

"Toby is too young to look after you."

"I know he is, and I don't expect him to look after me. I'll look after him. But on days when the migraines are bad, he's old enough to watch YouTube and keep himself entertained. We'll be fine. Remember I traveled with him when he was much more dependent on me."

I was not surprised by the grilling I got from my parents. I'd come to accept that this came from a place of love. They were concerned because they cared; it was their way of saying 'we love you.' What did surprise me was their level of interest and involvement from that moment on. Once they'd come to terms with the fact that this was what I needed, and that I'd done thorough research into how the whole thing worked, they developed an enthusiasm for the project. Of course, I didn't think of it as just a project, but they liked the thought that after a year, if it wasn't working out, I would come home and start my life over. I, on the other hand, never thought of it as a trip with an end. From the very start, I felt that it was a lifestyle change for me and Toby.

By May, I had booked the first leg of our trip. We were going to be starting at the World School Family Summit held by Lainie Liberti and her now adult son Miro in Granada, Spain. There we would spend two weeks with other World School families. We'd make connections and learn more about world schooling. Toby and I were so excited. The months couldn't pass quickly enough.

Actually, correction. With hindsight, they passed far too quickly. Before I knew it, we were on our way. I had a buyer for my business, and then that fell through, ultimately leading to me giving my clients notice of the closure of the business. That left me feeling bereft. In July, when I cleared out my office for the last time, I realized that, in a way, I was losing my reason for being. The place where I buried myself and my thoughts for up to 15 hours a day. I suddenly felt lost, scared, and overwhelmingly sad for what I'd lost on the 7th of September, 2015. For the first time, I was going to have time to face my life for what it was. I was afraid of having the time to mourn the life I'd had and crave days without pain, days when my mind was clear and lucid, and I took things like the ability to read for granted.

I was exhausted, overwhelmed, and sleep deprived. I couldn't wait to slow down, to take time to heal, but I was also troubled by the prospect. I'd sounded confident when speaking to my parents, but deep down, I was worried. At this stage of my life, I should have been working toward my retirement. I knew that. I also knew that I was no longer capable of doing that. I had nightmares about Toby becoming an uneducated wild man with no sense of responsibility. I had the house to pack up; we were moving out on the 14th of September, then there was Toby's birthday to arrange, travel insurance to purchase, goodbyes to be said, and bags to be packed.

Traveling economically meant that we'd each be allowed one carry on bag weighing no more than 20 kilograms. Anything more would be costly, so just deciding what stayed and what went was a feat on its own. It was a whirlwind of organization.

The migraines were still bad, but their frequency had reduced after I stopped working in July. I was still wrestling with nightmares, but something big happened in the month of September. My 'bouncing eyes' steadied. I was able to read more easily. This was a major breakthrough. Not every day was the same, but the words just shivered and stretched a bit instead of bouncing on the page. It was more than I'd hoped for, and within just two months of giving up working, it boded well for recovery over time. Suddenly, I was no longer as scared as I had been, and the nightmares became less frequent.

Chapter 11:

The World is Our Oyster

My dad got Toby and me to the airport in Toronto in plenty of time on the 1st of October. After hugs and kisses, he headed back to my mom and life in Kawartha Lakes, and Toby and I were left in excited anticipation of the rest of our lives.

We checked in our luggage and chose to have dinner at Boccone Trattoria Veloce, an Italian restaurant, in honor of our new adventurous lifestyle. With our adjusted slimline budget in mind, we opted for a light meal. The crispy sourdough bruschetta that I ordered with tomato salsa, basil, and parmesan cheese was delicious, and the portion was not too small. Toby tucked into Patatine Fritte, crispy potato fries with rosemary salt and a fontina cheese dip. Yum.

On board the plane, we discovered that half the seats weren't booked, so after take-off, we moved further apart, spread ourselves out, stretched out luxuriously over three seats each, and had a sleep. I wiggled a bit to try and get my shoulder comfortable; falling asleep in any old place or position was no longer as easy as it had been, but I eventually fell asleep. I woke to the sensation of falling out of bed. The airplane shook, dropped, then steadied. Another lurch downwards had me scrambling to a seated position as the intercom pinged and the seatbelt sign lit up. I looked across the aisle to Toby. He was already seated upright, and looking quite pale. One more big bump, and his Patatine Fritte spewed over the carpet and the back of the seat in front of him.

It took all my self control to clean up without adding to the mess myself. The flight attendants disappeared like mist before the sun. Other, better prepared moms stepped in, digging out wipes and tissues from their handbags. Toby looked pinched and contrite, tears shimmering in his eyes.

"Hey, it's okay," I said to him, giving his leg a squeeze.

"Happens all the time. Even to grown men," one mom said kindly.

After a general clean up, Toby was relieved to escape to fresher smelling seats. Another mom nearby, clearly a frequent flier with kids, came over and offered me some Gravol to ease Toby's nausea. I buzzed for the stewardess to bring a plastic cup of water for Toby to swallow them with. By then the turbulence was over, but Toby stayed nauseous, a puke bag at the ready, his forehead slicked with sweat. My poor boy.

We arrived in Barcelona feeling a little worse for wear. The ground crew were even less helpful than the flight crew had been. I couldn't find anyone who could assist us in finding our connection to Granada, and to add to the mayhem, security officials made me pass through the metal detector five times. Why? I don't know. The thing hadn't been set off, unless there was a silent buzzer somewhere. Nobody explained. I just kept getting waved back again and again. My bag went through the X-ray machine four times, I was patted down, and my bag was swabbed twice. All this time Toby was seated on the ground, sheet white and sweating profusely, his puke bag at the ready.

My patience wore thin, as I wondered what had singled me out for this attention. Was it because I wasn't traveling with a man? Because I had a nose piercing, or a tattoo? Oddly, the more they checked, scanned, and patted, the more nervous I became. I knew there was nothing dangerous or illegal in my bag or on my person, but I couldn't help it. The suspicion in their eyes was enough to make me start questioning myself. Had someone tampered with my bag? Impossible, I carried it on. Had I left it unattended at the airport while we had dinner or I went to the washroom? By the time I was finally allowed to move on and board the next flight, I was both angry and anxious.

We landed in Granada 20 minutes early and were still feeling unsettled. Toby hadn't thrown up again, but only because there was nothing left inside of him. He was still pale and clammy. I opted not to wait for the bus, but to take a cab to the Airbnb. When we arrived, I realized that I hadn't brought the owner's number with me. Fortunately, a woman entering the building assisted us in near perfect English, and even buzzed our apartment and acted as a translator for us.

We were met at the apartment by our hostess, a very gracious lady, who had laid out a welcoming tray of local olive oil, olives, and fruit. She even walked us down to the local bakery and bought us a loaf of stone baked bread. Then on to the grocery store, where she helped me pick out some amazing chorizo (a cured Spanish sausage), both picante (spicy) and dulce (sweet). The walk seemed to be good for Toby, and by the time we got back to the apartment with our loot, both his color and his appetite had returned. We cut thick slices of bread, drizzled them with olive oil, and topped them with slices of rich, garlicky smoked sausage. Delicious. We nibbled on soft, rich, slightly bitter black olives in between, then rounded off the meal with sweet-tart and very juicy Valencia oranges.

Bellies full, we turned in for a good sleep. We'd been on the go for 36 hours, and as exciting as it was to be in our first foreign country, we needed the battery recharge to prepare for the adventures to come.

Despite having (according to Toby, I'm a technological disaster) 25Gb of Google Maps on our phone, and taking care to remember landmarks, we spent a lot of time getting lost. Toby found it very funny. "We're going to spend most of the next year wandering around, lost in foreign countries," he remarked with a laugh. You would think that, on foot, you're going slowly enough to absorb your surroundings and that it's hard to get lost. But nope. It was easy. Far too easy. We sure got a lot of exercise, though.

We enjoyed wandering the streets of Spain and admiring the old architecture, mostly Moorish. The Alhambra, a medieval palace (initially built as a fortress in 889, and later converted to a royal residence) was a spectacular example of blended architecture combining Moorish Islamic and Christian aesthetics. Covering an area of 142,000 square meters, it was enormous, more of a citadel or walled city than a building, with intricate lattice work, filigreed walls, frescoes, and columns. It was a work of art and an engineering feat. We found it hard to imagine how, without technology, cranes, and other engineering advances, it had been possible. If that wasn't mind blowing enough, the intricate artistic detail was like nothing we'd ever seen before.

In the streets, the people all seemed so busy, at times even rude. I commented on this to Toby. "Have you noticed how people are all so absorbed in their phones? They hardly look up." I couldn't imagine being so distracted; even beneath our feet, the sidewalks were beautiful cobblestone mosaics. I wondered whether the locals appreciated the beauty they trod on every day. Everything was fascinating.

"Kind of. But I think it's not so different to home. Maybe now that you aren't so busy, you are more aware of it?"

His insight surprised me. But it made sense. Not entirely confident yet with the 'world schooling system' on its own, I'd bought the Grade 6 curriculum before we left, as a kind of 'back-up plan.' So, between exploratory trips and gastronomic experiences, Toby was still working on his traditional homework. The progress was slower than I'd have liked, but this was a step closer to 'world schooling,' which is very much learner directed.

When we weren't exploring or working on the curriculum, we met up with other 'world school' families who were gathering in Granada for the summit that was due to start on the 14th of October. We were fascinated by their stories, mostly exciting and adventurous, and some borderline scary!

On the 8th, news reached us in Spain of the tragic death of Devan Selvey, a Canadian child stabbed in the back by school bullies within sight of his mother, who had gone to collect him from school. My heart broke for his mother. Apparently, he'd been afraid to go to school after numerous bullying incidents, some quite violent, but she'd encouraged him. The school principal had been giving her a hard time about Devan's attendance, which was poor due to his fear. I could only imagine her pain. She too was a single mom, and Devan must have been her world. Two of the three students that hadn't actually wielded the knife were being allowed to return to school to attend classes alongside Devan's friends, who had also been bullied by them. I felt sick. The school system had once again failed another innocent child. The PTSD reared its ugly head in a big way, bringing me horrible nightmares of bullying from my school days and Toby's.

On the same day that the 'world schooling' summit started in the south of Spain, violent protests broke out in Catalonia to the north east, shutting down roads, airports, and stations. Catalonians were demanding the release of nine separatist leaders who had been sentenced that morning for their part in a failed 2017 independence bid. It was a hot topic; it seems every country has its problems. These leaders had been sentenced to between 9 and 13 years in prison.

Note: at the time of publishing this book, roughly 16 months after these events, one of the accused in Devan Selvey's murder, an 18-year-old, had been sentenced to 15 months of probation. The other, the 14-year-old that wielded the knife, was due to stand trial for a reduced charge of second degree murder. I still can't stop thinking of his poor mother, and how society failed her and her son. The disparity between this political crime in Spain and the horrendous murder in Canada troubled me. Where are our values? Is power more important than life?

The summit was incredible. We met so many people from all over the world who traveled and educated their children. We had dinner with David and Junco, an Australian/Japanese couple who shared a wealth of knowledge of Japan. We also met up with an Italian family with three kids for a day in the park. She was a photographer, and he, an energy healer, both of whom had done presentations at the summit.

Toby made new friends from the UK, Australia, Denmark, Sweden, the US, and other countries. One of the parents started a special chat site specifically for traveling children as a safe platform for them to connect outside of traditional social media outlets. One of the teens was into 'coding,' and working on developing a new game. He spent some time with Toby teaching him the basics of 'code.'

Things started to happen quickly, and our itinerary started to take shape. We met Luna Vestergaard and her three children from Denmark. They invited us to spend Christmas at their home in northern Denmark. I booked for ten days in Athens, and then a two week tour in Egypt with other world schooling families, followed by another three days in Athens with 2 families from the Egypt tour. From Athens, we would head north towards our Christmas destination.

We hiked the hanging bridges of Monachil with Armando Hevia and his two kids and Inge with her daughter, both of whom we'd met at the summit. It was not for the faint of heart, or the 'out of shape.' Toby loved it and didn't seem to share my fear of heights. He had us in stitches when he decided to try an olive off the tree; the extreme bitterness was visible on his screwed up face for about 40 minutes, during which time he ate endless slices of bread and downed copious cups of water.

We landed in Athens at 10 o'clock at night on the 3rd of November and were collected by our Airbnb host as arranged. Toby and I were starving, and decided at around 10:30 to venture out and grab a sandwich at the nearest corner restaurant. We walked home quickly afterwards, feeling a bit uncomfortable in the neighborhood.

The next morning, we headed out in daylight. We found a wonderful bakery where Toby bought a donut and we ate sweet-crispy-buttery-citrusy-nutty baklava for breakfast. In Canada, Greek restaurants tend to serve baklava as a desert. In Greece, it holds more importance and is served as a sweet treat on high days and holidays like weddings, Christmas, and Easter.

Once we'd licked our fingers clean, we looked for the Parthenon on Google Maps.

Google Maps, oblivious to the fact that it was guiding a single woman and an 11-year-old boy, led us through a park filled with addicts in various stages of highs and lows. We picked our way between strewn garbage and drug-related paraphernalia. The addicts took little notice of me, but some of them tried to catch Toby's attention, making eye contact, and calling out. I'm not sure which of the two of us were more freaked out. We kept our heads down and walked on, while I explained to Toby that Greece had run into huge financial trouble in 2010, but because their financial woes would affect the viability of the eurozone (all the countries that had a adopted the Euro), various European governments and private individuals had lent Greece hundreds of billions of Euros to keep them going. The problem was that these loans came with conditions: austerity measures. The government had to increase taxes, wages were cut, and unemployment grew.

"Many people turned to drugs or alcohol to avoid the reality of losing their jobs and homes."

"I understand, Mom, but there has to be another way. They have to make it possible for everyone to have a home and not live like this!" He was horrified. As uncomfortable as we were walking through that area, it had opened Toby's eyes to the suffering of others, and how much we take for granted. It felt surreal exiting the park and entering the tourist areas, where restaurants were filled with well-dressed, clean people, laughing, eating, and taking photographs. It truly was a tale of two cities. It reminded me of our trip to the two Nogales' in Mexico and the USA. I reminded Toby of this, and ignited a discussion about the extremes of wealth and poverty that exist all over the world, and how one person's 'normal' can be so disparate from another's, even within the same country.

The following morning, Toby wanted another donut. "I'll pay for it with my allowance, Mom."

"Maybe later, okay? I'm not ready yet." I was still in my sleepshirt, and not enthused about getting dressed and walking the two blocks to the bakery.

"I'll go by myself. It's not far."

I paused, considering this. We were in a strange country, and Toby had always been at my side, even in Canada. Was I being overprotective? He was, after all, 11 years old. Eventually, I gave in, but couldn't help watching out the window as he made his way to the bakery and back. My boy was growing up. It became his morning habit to slip out to the bakery, allowance in hand, in the morning for one of those amazing donuts, and after a day or two, I stopped watching out the window and trusted that he'd return, safe and happy with a big sugary grin.

We managed to work out how to use the Greek metro and bus lines, and headed to the beach where we met up with an American family who had two children in Toby's age group. The kids spent the whole day swimming in the Aegean Sea. I mentioned that it had been a relief to discover that the metro was not as complicated as I'd first thought, so was no longer stressing as much about getting to the airport on Saturday. My cheeky son responded, "Yeah, at least this time we won't have to leave our Airbnb 21 hours before flight time due to Mommy's nerves!"

Toby was dreading the next flight, having suffered from crippling airsickness on several flights so far. As a qualified hypnotherapist, I thought this might be the time to put my money where my mouth was. I'd been qualified for almost 20 years, but never gone into it full time because of my own self-doubt. I suffered from impostor syndrome in a big way. Probably because I'd heard from so many people that it was just a bunch of mumbo-jumbo. I found it hard to reconcile my two worlds. As Toby wasn't a paying client, though, I reckoned we had nothing to lose. In our Airbnb, I guided Toby through a hypnosis session, focusing on how he felt when he traveled by air. It paid off big time. Toby never threw up on another flight.

We landed in Egypt at 11:11 a.m. I believe that the number 11 is significant in our lives, and that we need to pay attention to numbers that appear in this manner. It was even more relevant when Toby and I had our photograph taken standing in front of the pyramids of Giza holding hands. Toby was 11 years old; it was the 11th day of the 11 month, and I now had a physical photograph of the image that had appeared so often to me in my dreams when I was pregnant.Egypt was a whirlwind tour in 13 days. It started with the pyramids of Giza, then on to the Philae Temples. We did a cruise on the Nile, 2 camel rides, ATVs through the desert, dune buggies in the desert, a Bedouin village 25 kms into the desert, Abu Simbel Temples, Luxor, Aswan, NassarLake, Karnak Temple, markets, shops, the Red Sea and dolphins and coral reefs, the museum of Cairo, the Temple of Hatshepsut, and the Valley of the Kings.

Two things that stand out most from that crazy two weeks of Egyptian immersion are:

Firstly, the Abu Simbel Temples, the most amazing two temples carved from a massive sandstone cliff commissioned by King Ramses II in the 1200s BC. If we'd thought the Alhambra was an impressive feat for its time, this was hard to comprehend. Figures of Rameses (seated on a throne), carved from stone, stood 20 meters high.

The other was at Nassar Lake. It was hot, humid, and dusty, so dusty that the sand seemed to drift just like snow. The lake itself, we were told, is one of the world's biggest man-made reservoirs; 90 meters deep and 22 kilometers wide. The total area of the lake was about 5250 square kilometers! It looked stunning, and in the sweltering conditions, the water was incredibly inviting. Our guide warned us, "Never swim here, no matter how hot you are or how beautiful it looks. An average of one person per day dies here every day. Killed by crocodiles. There are between 20 and 30 thousand crocodiles that can't get up the Nile because of the Aswan Dam, and they have taken over this lake."

Thank goodness for our guides. We felt that tourists were seen as wealthy, and vendors on the streets were very pushy trying to make deals on the side. We were rescued from uncomfortable situations a number of times.

We were fascinated by the fact that Cairo was incredibly humid; our clothes just wouldn't dry, but on the shores of the Red Sea, there was no humidity. The poverty and the traffic were overwhelming. On the way to the airport, another vehicle side swiped the one we were traveling in, taking out the rear tail light, and scraping the vehicle right down the side. Toby and I were horrified, but neither vehicle stopped; the driver just shrugged it off as a normal part of daily commuting.

We returned to Athens for three days after leaving Cairo. This time, we shared a large Airbnb with Karen and her family. Karen was the lady who had arranged the tour of Egypt. Another traveling single mom, Nique, and her daughter also joined us. Having already done and seen a lot there, and after our packed schedule in Egypt, we were happy to take our time and relax. We ate more baklava; it really is quite addictive. We also discovered souvlaki; skewers of cubed pork marinated and basted with oregano, rosemary, garlic, and lemon and cooked over hot coals. This was particularly good dipped in tzatziki, a yogurt sauce with garlic and cucumber. It was the ultimate treat for those days when craving protein, and at less than two dollars, it was a treat we could afford!

We did a bus tour of Athens, and spent many happy hours at the Hellenic Motor Museum. Toby and I were both fascinated by the incredible collection of beautiful vehicles, from a 'Bedrock Buggy', built in 2381 BC, which had two big foot operated 'rollers,' to a gleaming purple Lamborghini, and everything in between. The museum is an often overlooked site for tourists in Athens, but an absolute 'must see' for any car enthusiast. It also slotted in well with his world schooling which is child directed. Toby being something of a petrolhead, was enthralled.

Arriving in Budapest, Hungary a couple days later, it was a bit of a shock to the system to find ourselves in cold wet weather. A relief after the heat and humidity of Egypt, but we weren't well-equipped for it, so we had to find a cheap clothing shop. We eventually found one that reminded me of the Bi-Way and Bargain Harold's discount stores we used to have in Canada in the 1980s. There we bought mitts and a toque for Toby.

We also had an interesting math lesson. My little math aficionado gets an allowance. He has since he was two years old. When he was two, he received $2 per week, at three, $3 per week etc. So, when we left Canada, as he was 11, he was receiving $11 a week. On arrival in Europe, the smart fellow decided that he should be getting 11 Euros a week; he even went so far as to start charging me interest when I didn't transfer the money into his account on the appointed date! So, imagine his surprise and my mirth when we arrived in Hungary and he only got 11 Hungarian Forints (worth about 5 Canadian cents)

We tested my fear for heights climbing the 172 steps to the top of Buda Tower, the restored bell tower of a now ruined 18th century church, which served as a mosque after the Turkish occupation of Budapest in 1686. The church was destroyed by an air raid in 1944. By the time we got back to the bottom, my knees were jelly, and it felt like an entire swarm of butterflies were causing havoc in my intestines.

A trip to the caves in the Buda hills was remarkable. Natural caves had existed beneath the streets of Buda Castle district, carved out by the subterranean water. These had been further excavated by locals, developing labyrinths, cellars, churches, and bunkers. These caves had provided great protection during the siege of Budapest around the end of World War II. There was even a functioning underground hospital, initially built to service less than a hundred people, and ultimately serving up to 600. This hospital, we were told later, became a nuclear bunker during the Cold War; the air raid siren is still there, as is other equipment, some of which remain functional.

Learning about the underground thermal waters that formed the original caves led us to our next logical step: enjoying an evening soaking in the mineral rich, healing thermal waters. It felt so luxurious to be enveloped in hot water; hot enough to make our cheeks turn pink while the steam rose into the chilly night air.

We also, quite literally, ate our way through the city. There were so many new and exciting foods to discover. Some of the most memorable include calorie laden langos: deep fried dough, topped with sour cream, garlic butter, cheese, and bacon. The bacon isn't really bacon as we know it in Canada and the US; it's fattier and salt cured or smoked, but you don't have to cook it again; it's a cold cut. We enjoyed the tangy-sweet-earthiness of borscht, a beetroot soup, served hot with a swirl of sour cream. We ate goulash, a simple but tasty paprika flavored meat stew; smoky Hungarian sausages served with sharp sauerkraut, and Toby's personal favorite: chimney cakes at the Christmas markets. Chimney cakes are tall hollow tubes of sweet yeast dough that are basted with butter while being cooked over coals. They are then rolled in sugar and stuffed with caramel cream and whipped cream. Super-indulgent, super-calorific, super-cheap, and super-delicious!

The Christmas market was festive and exquisite. The Europeans definitely know how to do Christmas, it is steeped in tradition, flavor, and color. There must have been about 100 market stalls around a tall Christmas tree, each one beautifully decorated, selling street food, beautifully crafted Christmas décor, and gifts with musical soirees in the evenings. I was almost tempted to indulge in a mulled wine, but decided that giving up alcohol was not something you sometimes do and sometimes don't.

Less fun, but even more important and necessary, was a visit to the Holocaust Memorial Museum. Toby's generation will be the first in the past 120 years to grow up without veterans of World Wars to remind them of the first hand horrific experiences of these wars and why we should never forget. We learned that although Hungary passed laws to suppress the Jews and their rights, the government of the time refused to turn them over to the Nazis for extermination. Until their invasion in March 1944. After this invasion, in a matter of 10 weeks, up to 90% of Hungarian Jews were captured and sent to Auschwitz-Birkenau. An estimated 400,000 to 600,000 people. It was terrifying, brutal, and torturous to know what humans did to their fellow men during the spring of 1944 in Hungary. That a person—someone's mother, father, brother, or sister—could be capable of inflicting such dreadful atrocities on people they didn't even know, blindly following orators and political leaders, cut deep. We saw photographs and film clips of real people who had been ripped from their families, humiliated, tortured, and ultimately murdered.

I expected this visit to be a moving experience, but had no idea of the depth of emotion it would trigger in me. I felt personally bereft, and struggled with tears the whole day. Toby too was pale and quiet. I vowed that, someday, I would take Toby to Auschwitz-Birkenau to ensure that the edict "Lest We Forget" and the full meaning behind it would become a part of his being on a deep level. But not yet. Despite my prior reading, the reality of it all was a shock, and it would take us days to process the horrors that the museum revealed.

On the 30th of November, we reluctantly left Hungary and traveled to Prague. The Czech language was completely foreign to us. In Hungary and Greece, when grocery shopping, we could usually find an English, Spanish, or Italian translation on products. In Czech, not so. We bought what looked like either pasta sauce or salsa, butter…or margarine…or cheese, something to drink that we hoped would be a soda or an energy drink (which fortunately didn't turn out to be an alcoholic cooler!).

We stopped for lunch, and standing at the café's service counter, had no idea how to order. We just pointed at the plates of the people in front of us, and with many giggles on both sides of the counter, were served bowls of steaming broth with chunks of potato and onion, and loads of garlic. Apparently, garlic soup is traditionally served as a hangover cure in Czechoslovakia; I don't know if it works or not, but it certainly was a delicious, cheap, and satisfying meal.

While we ate, Toby asked me if I could give him his allowance , so I dug in my purse and pulled out 11 Korunas and handed it over. He was quite happy until I explained that it was only worth about 63 Canadian cents. I laughed at the look of shock on his face, and even harder at his expression when I added, "I can't wait until we get to Thailand; 11 Bhat is worth 48 cents!"

I was teasing him, of course, but it was a great learning experience for him, realizing just how much more fortunate we were than so many others in the world. I was serious about going to Thailand, though, and the next day I booked our flights to Thailand for January. I still had no idea where we would stay yet, and reached out to other traveling families for recommendations.

We had met Susanna and Niclas Nilsson at the summit in Spain. They were a Swedish couple who had moved to Prague in order to be allowed to remove their children from conventional schooling. Their son was a few months younger than Toby, and their daughter a little older than him. As it turned out, our Airbnb in Prague was conveniently just 6 blocks from their apartment. We spent a lovely day at the zoo with Susanna and the kids. It was cold, very cold, in Prague, and we hadn't packed nearly enough winter clothing. The zoo was home to a wide variety of animals, including polar bears and various African animals such as giraffes, elephants, and hippos. Toby and I couldn't help wondering whether the African animals were feeling the cold too.

On another occasion, we met up with the Nilssons on a long evening walk to the Charles Bridge to see the lighting of the lamps. Charles Bridge is the only gaslit bridge in the world. In the run up to Christmas, a man comes out in medieval dress and walks the bridge, lighting the many gas lamps with a long rod topped with a burning wick. The rest of the year, the lights are turned on by automatic switch. Toby was honored to be one of the lucky visitors singled out to assist with lighting a lamp.

We were invited to a couple of meals at the Nilssons'. One of them was a fabulous Swedish spread, to which they had invited another Canadian 'world schooling' couple, the Tullis'. We loved the Swedish meatballs, small balls of ground beef spiced with nutmeg and allspice in a creamy sauce, and all the salads and vegetables. We were a little less sure of the salted licorice candies, and decided that they were an acquired taste. Both the Nillson and Tullis families very kindly loaned us some warmer clothing, which allowed us to venture beyond our Airbnb without fear of frostbite. At dinner, the conversation turned to how different people celebrate Christmas, and Toby was fascinated by the differences. Where we usually think of Christmas as a time of giving, and our Christmas 'characters' (outside of the religious) consisted of a jolly Santa in a red suit, and cute little elves making toys for all the good children around the world, in Prague, there was a 'dark side' that was celebrated pre-Christmas. They told us about Krampus, a monster that was half-goat, half-demon that walked the streets and punished naughty children, beating them with sticks; really bad children were stolen away from their parents and served up as dinner for Krampus! They told us that there would be a Krampus Parade the following evening.

After our dinner with the Nilsson family, we took their advice and attended the Krampus Parade with the Tullis'. The costumes were spectacular, loads of half-demon, half-goat characters with horns, fur, and evil grimacing skull-like faces walked and danced down the street, snatching hats off people, posing for selfies, and grabbing children and walking off with them. The children shrieked in mock horror. I was glad that we knew something of the history of this pagan festival when a Krampus grabbed Toby from over the barrier and started walking off with him. Anyone not knowing what was happening might have thought they'd found themselves in their worst nightmare! Even knowing that it was all an act, I found myself shivering at the hideousness of some of the players, and jumping at some blood-curdling screams. Toby very calmly allowed himself to be led away by Krampus; I decided I needed to have the 'stranger danger' talk with him again.

Before heading to Denmark to stay with Luna and her family, Toby and I visited with Lucia Gomez and her three sons, one of whom was Toby's age. They too were 'world schoolers' based in a small town about 40 kilometers from Bratislava. It was a five-day visit to the economic and political hub of Slovakia. We explored the Bratislava Castle on a rocky hill overlooking the Danube. The second floor houses the Slovak National Museum, which gave us a good insight into the culture and history of the area. But we were so cold, it was hard to concentrate. Our cheeks were burning. We eventually ventured out to street food park, a monthly pop up of food stalls in front of the Old Market Hall in search of something warm to eat. We were surprised to find loads of hamburgers, hot dogs, and Mexican food on offer, and had to search hard to find authentic traditional food. Eventually, we settled on potato pancakes for Toby and potato dumplings (very similar to gnocchi) with goat's milk cheese for me. The meal was interesting, but not as exciting as the flavors we'd experienced in Hungary. For much of the rest of our time there, we holed up inside against the cold.

We both agreed that it would be nice to visit Eastern Europe again, in warmer weather, or with the right clothing. We were sure we could have seen and done more if we'd been better prepared.

From Prague, we headed to Lønstrup, Denmark, for Christmas with Luna, who was also hosting another 'world schooling' family from Australia, Sarah Beale, her husband, two sons, and two daughters. Once a quaint fishing village, it is probably better known these days as the setting for the Danish film Babette's Feast. In reality, it is a tiny village inhabited by artsy crafty folk. Toby was most impressed by the glass blowers and potters, while I was fascinated at the jewellery and amber crafters. So much talent in such a small place. It was fun to experience the excitement of the Beales experiencing their first ever winter in the Northern Hemisphere. Their pure joy and childlike wonder was the gilt edge to our own.

The Beale's had a large van, and one day invited us to join them on a day trip to the northernmost point of Denmark, about an hour's drive from Lønstrup. There we took a walk on the beach, where Toby got to put his hands in two seas at once. His left hand was in the North Sea, and his right in the Baltic Sea. We didn't swim, firstly because it was too cold, and secondly because of the opposing currents that make swimming conditions dangerous. It was most unusual; we could clearly see a line of foam where the two seas meet but apparently don't mix.

Christmas was beautiful, with real candles on the Christmas tree, and a wonderful meal of roast pork, duck, and rice pudding, Risalamande, with a hidden almond that if found in your bowl qualified you for an extra gift. Luna was a wonderful hostess, warm and genuine, and I was sorry when the time came for us to leave. I know, though, that the friendship that blossomed there was one of those forever ones, the kind that can go months without contact and be picked up again as if no time had passed at all.

Chapter 12:

Stretching Boundaries Before the Pandemic

On the 31st of December, Toby and I held hands as we literally flew into the new year at 37,000 feet. We were leaving the warm hospitality and cold climes of Denmark as we headed for Thailand.

We landed in Krabi and exited the airplane to a blast of 34-degree Celsius heat exacerbated by 70% humidity. We took the airport bus to the town, and hungry, decided to grab a bite to eat before heading to our 'resort'—a term I use loosely. We bought fish cakes that were served on a bamboo skewer from a street vendor. After one bite, we both had tears streaming down our faces and were looking around urgently for bread or milk—neither of which were near at hand. We soldiered on, wiping our cheeks and sniffing between bites. We needed to learn the words for hot and spicy in Thai, and quickly, or we were going to go hungry! With a bit of research on Google, we discovered that by saying mai ped, we could avoid further mouth blistering. Mai meaning 'no,' and ped, 'spicy.'

We flagged down a songthaew, a kind of mini truck that acts as a bus, and traveled to a hostel, recommended by fellow travelers. We sat facing each other on benches on the back of the truck, and there was a string attached to a buzzer that we had to pull to tell the driver to stop. The traffic and driving were erratic, but transport was cheap. The hostel was clean, budget friendly, and not so comfortable; sharp bed springs made sleep a little hard to come by. But, it was close to the reclining Buddha about halfway between Krabi and AoNang Beach.

I was probably not the best company for Toby the first three days. I was struck by a migraine that just wouldn't budge. I couldn't stay in bed, though, both because the bedsprings made it a painful pastime and because I didn't want to keep Toby cooped up in the hostel, or let him go exploring on his own.

We were once again awed by the beauty of our surroundings. Towering, chalky, limestone karst cliffs, soft white beach sand, and calm waters in stunning shades of turquoise. This was, we decided, paradise. We visited the reclining Buddha, a gold-colored statue about 15 meters high and 46 meters long, gleaming in the sun against a backdrop of enormous cliffs covered in green vegetation. I couldn't face the more than 1200 steps to the Tiger Cave temple, so we decided to put that off for another day.

Then we packed up, and took another songthaew, and a ferry, to the island of Koh Lanta. There we were booked into a 'resort' for a month. It was more like a few bungalows in the middle of a coconut plantation. The important thing was that it was cute, quaint, suited our budget, and didn't have poky bedsprings. Actually, there were no bedsprings at all. Toby's 'bed' was a piece of plywood on the floor with two sheets folded under him as padding. Mine was a concrete slab, with a folded comforter between me and the cement.

It was also a little bit frightening. The bathroom was open to the outdoors (and the monkeys). At night, monkeys sometimes clambered over the roof, keeping us entertained, and inside! Those monkeys, as cute as they were, had sharp teeth and strong wills. One day, Toby and I watched as a tourist was accosted by a monkey while walking home with his bag of groceries. The monkey ran up to him, stood up on its hind legs, and grabbed at the bag. A tugging match ensued, which the tourist only won by stamping his feet and shouting.

A couple of times, I found rat poop in the bathroom. After a few days there, as Toby and I were getting ready for bed, we spotted the culprit, skirting our 'bedroom' looking for crumbs. He was HUGE. I screamed and leapt onto my concrete slab, and Toby, prompted by my shrieks, scrambled up next to me. I'm not sure who got the bigger fright, because the rat paused, looked at us, and then took off into the bathroom, leaving Toby and I in fits of nervous giggles. Back under control, I followed the rat to the bathroom and was just in time to see its tail disappearing as it scooted down a drainpipe. I stuffed an upside down bottle of shampoo into the drainpipe, but the next day, there was fresh evidence of rat poop in the bathroom. I retrieved the shampoo bottle and stuffed a towel into the pipe instead. The next day, returning from the beach, we found more droppings, and gave up. We learned instead to live with our new pet. He was a creature of habit, turning up at the same time every evening and sniffing around for food before disappearing outside again. Fortunately, he never got into our beds, or at least if he did, he was polite enough not to mess on them, or join us as we slept.

Staying in cheaper accommodations meant that we were quite far from the beach, so I elected to hire a scooter to get around on. This was rather hair raising, even for me as an experienced motorbike rider. The scooter had a short wheel base, which made riding it different to riding a bike; also, the traffic was chaotic and on the opposite side of the road as Canada. To add to the challenges, I had to constantly use my peripheral vision as monkeys were wont to suddenly sprint across the road in a death defying bid to reach the other side.

On one day, Toby and I traveled to the top of a cliff to admire the view and enjoy a frozen lemonade. The lemonade was delicious, neither too sweet nor too sour, and perfect for a hot day. Later that evening, I rode out to the beachfront to pick up a take out dinner for us (mai pad of course!). Toby, taking strain from the heat, had decided to stay at the bungalow. I sat alone on the beach while the food was prepared, and thought about our travels. Were we learning enough? We were sure using up a lifetime's worth of adrenaline.

I sat with my toes buried in the warm sand and marvelled at the number of times we'd been outside of our comfort zones during our travels. Later, after our travels, when I mentioned this to Lainie, she had said, "Life is like three large circles, one inside the next, inside the next. The smallest inside circle is our comfort zone, where we like to be; it's safe and filled with familiarity and routine. The next large circle isn't fully outside of the comfort zone; it's only a little out, and this is your 'stretch' zone. This is where growth happens and is often the best place to live life from. The final largest circle is outside of your comfort zone. It's your fear zone. This is the zone that it's best to avoid if and when you can, but if you're familiar with your stretch zone, it won't be nearly as uncomfortable for you as it would if you only know your comfort zone."

Of course, we hadn't had that discussion yet as I sat on the beach in the setting sun, but I was very aware of how many new experiences we were having, and how much braver I was feeling about setting out into the unknown.

Shortly thereafter, the universe provided us with a free, but depressing, lesson on the importance of environmental conservation. There had been a storm the previous night, and the water was a bit rough. These rougher seas brought sharp shards of coral in varying sizes to the beach. We found it difficult to dodge all the coral strewn across the sand, the bigger pieces the size of a football. Continuing our walk, we eventually reached a coral graveyard—thousands of pieces of dead coral. It was heartbreaking. Because the north beach was littered with debris and jellyfish, we headed to the south beach to see if it had escaped the same fate. We were excited to see that it had, and ran into the water. We must have swum, floated, and played for about an hour before I noticed an odd line across the water in the distance, about 100 meters out and parallel with the horizon. We watched as it came closer. Others saw it too, and started exiting the water. Toby and I, realizing that this was something the others were probably familiar with, and not comfortable with, also headed for the shore, and stood in ankle deep water to see what it was. As it approached, it was clear that it was debris, only this time it wasn't just twigs, leaves, seaweed, and jellyfish; it was interspersed with human garbage. Almost all of it plastic. We joined the locals in collecting floating plastic bottles and bags and putting them into bins.

There was worse to come; along with the debris came a dark, oily slick of film on the water. It was gross. It stuck to the bathing suits of those still in the water. Toby's air mattress was coated with it. It didn't appear to be oil, nor sewage; I don't know what it was, but it bubbled strangely and clung to everything. We ended up leaving the beach early, disturbed by the damage man was doing to the earth. We talked at length about the small changes that people desperately needed to start making before it was too late. Being careful what you put down your drains and reducing plastic usage. It was apparent that modern technology was focused on manufacturing, but not on filtering the waste it produced.

About 10 days prior to my 50th birthday, Toby and I explored underwater caves, swimming 80 meters through one. What an amazing experience. We stuck close together, though, remembering the 12 young football players and their coach who had been trapped in one of these caves by floodwaters some 18 months prior.

Two days later, Toby and I were on the scooter after dark, heading for dinner in Old Town Koh Lanta. Road construction had caused excess dust, and a truck had recently dumped water on the road to settle it. This made the road treacherously slippery, and coming around a corner, the wheels just slid out from under us. I crashed to the ground with the scooter trapping my one leg. My first panicked thought was for Toby, but before I could even look around for him, he was there, lifting the scooter from my leg and grabbing me under my shoulders to pull me up.

We struggled upright and pulled the scooter off the road as fast as we could. Thai traffic is *very* fast, and we were in a rush to get out of the way. My flimsy shorts were covered in wet mud; in fact, at first when I stood up, I thought I'd lost them while sliding along the road. I grabbed at my butt and was comforted to feel the fabric through the mud. We gathered our scattered goods and a broken piece from the scooter. I was shaking with shock, putting weight on my right leg hurt like hell, and a burning, stinging sensation in my right thigh made me look. Blood seeped from a cut. Toby was shaken, and his butt cheek was black and blue, but other than that, we seemed to be okay.

After about 10 minutes of just standing there, letting the adrenaline settle, we got back on the bike and headed back to our bungalow for damage control. After about half an hour of scrubbing and soaking, Toby was starving, so we got back on the scooter and headed to Bamboo Restaurant, a friendly, family run concern.

Some Swedish people we'd befriended were there, and within minutes of our arrival, they and the restaurant owners, including an 80-year-old mama with more than 50 years' experience doing body work, were assessing my leg and ensuring that Toby was okay. I had been coping fine until this point, but suddenly, no longer having to hold it together, and with the shock wearing off, I burst into tears and had a complete meltdown. Lars, one of our Swedish friends, drove me to the pharmacy where the pharmacist pronounced that there might be a fracture, but if there was, it wasn't serious. I asked for Ibuprofen, and she said, "Not strong enough; take these." She handed me Tramadol without a prescription!

Back at the restaurant, the locals told us not to go for an x-ray. "Hospital machine old and dangerous. Clinic open on Monday. Safe machine there; go Monday." Once Toby had eaten, we rode 'home,' where I lay in extreme discomfort and wished for sleep. Either that or a whiskey. It had been four and a half years since I'd given up drinking, and I've never wished for a whiskey that badly. It was a restless night, and at one o'clock in the morning, I was performing a full hour of Reiki on my screaming leg. The next day, we returned to the Bamboo Restaurant for food again, and Mama massaged my leg. It was incredibly painful, but by the time she was finished, my leg felt bruised but no longer in agony. Toby was stiff, but other than that, we'd gotten off lightly.

Fortunately, our bodies recovered well, and by the 28th of January, my 50th birthday, Toby and I were strong enough to celebrate with a cable ride on the Koh Lanta zipline. I say this casually, but I have an intense fear of heights. I decided that the best way to celebrate my arrival at 'mid-life' would be to face that fear head on by launching myself into mid-air over the jungles of Koh Lanta. The sea views were jaw-dropping—when I was brave enough to open my eyes. My jaw wasn't the only thing that dropped; with every leap of faith on those lines, my stomach dropped too. Talk about pushing boundaries and getting out of your comfort zone. My heart was racing by the time we reached the 13th and final platform. I was shaking but proud. Toby was a little more nonchalant in his excitement; he either didn't share my fear of heights, or his pride was stronger than his fear.

The following day, we bade our bungalow and its rat a fond farewell, and took the ferry from Koh Lanta to Phuket, then a flight to Hanoi in Vietnam. The atmosphere at the airport was very different to when we'd arrived. News of a contagious and deadly virus that had been identified in Wuhan was abounding, and everyone seemed to be regarding everyone else with suspicion. People wore masks covering their noses and mouths. Restaurants stood empty, because nobody wanted to remove their mask to eat or drink. A cough or a sneeze caused a wave of people moving away from the offending person. The news was scary and confusing. There appeared to be a few thousand people who'd contracted this flu-like virus, but a province of 50 million were being placed under quarantine. Something wasn't adding up. Either the numbers coming out of China were lower than the reality, or the media was overdoing the hype. Whatever the truth was, people were afraid.

After the relatively chill Thai island life (I never thought I'd say that about Thai traffic), the streets of Hanoi were overwhelming. Horns honked loudly, and cars, trucks, and scooters seemed to miss each other by a hair's breadth as they zipped manically along. One look at this lot told me I wouldn't be driving here.

We were hungry again. We always seemed to be hungry! Our hotel recommended a restaurant on the corner. We walked there. There were more scooters parked outside our hotel than we'd seen on the entire island of Koh Lanta. We were a bit perplexed when we reached the corner and found no recognizable restaurant. Just some plastic chairs and tables grouped on the sidewalk and a person at a stall cooking noodles and veggies. I looked at Toby and said, "I have no idea how this works. What have I got us into?"

He shrugged and said, "Your idea, not mine, Mom."

We sat at an empty table and waited, unsure whether we were supposed to wait for service, or to up and order. We watched and waited. We were served; I still don't know if this was the correct procedure, or just the vendor recognizing our tourist status. A smiling young girl came to take our order. We had no idea what to order, or how to order it, so we looked around and pointed at someone else's table. She smiled again, then walked away. Ten minutes later, we were savouring delicious hot noodles with bok choy and beef and lemon tea. We ate slowly, enjoying every bite as we watched and listened to the world shoot past as if on speed.

We walked everywhere we went. We quickly learned that when crossing a road, if you keep a steady pace, the scooters swerve around you, but cars don't. You have to wait for a gap between cars and hot foot it. We saw three Ferraris in one day, making Toby think that they weren't that expensive. He was enticed by all the knock off designer gear, and said, "Next time we come, I need to bring an empty suitcase to fill up. There's so much cool stuff!"

We escaped the frenetic traffic by strolling through a park and visiting Hoan Kiem Lake. We watched the famous water puppet show, where puppeteers, hidden behind a screen, performed with puppets on sticks that appeared to float across the water. Toby loved it; I was less enamoured by the actual show, but entranced by the music played on instruments that I didn't recognize.

After Hanoi, we spent three days in DaNang. There we discovered how violent and unpredictable the South China Sea is. Unlike the Pacific and Atlantic oceans, which had some rhythm or pattern to the waves, the waves there were huge, erratic, and totally unpredictable. There was a vast, beautiful beach, but swimming was severely restricted to a very small roped off area with several lifeguards watching over. A dip in the ocean with Toby soon had us realizing how important this was. It involved more of a struggle to stay upright than actually swimming, and we were dumped unceremoniously onto the sand a number of times by the massive waves before eventually giving up.

We visited the Marble Mountains just outside of DaNang, and toured the Heaven and Hell caves. There we met an American lawyer, Herb, and were glad to have his company. We crossed a stone bridge over a pond from which carved hands reached out, begging for salvation, then entered a cave, *Am Phu*; this is a Buddhist depiction of hell. It was dark, with eerie red and sometimes green lighting, and filled with sculptures of demons and people being beaten and tortured. Masks portrayed expressions of intense anger and horror. It was like entering the tunnel of horrors at a fun fair. You know it's not real, but the atmosphere is enough to make you jumpy. In between some of the ghoulish statues, we discovered a few live creepy crawlies. Toby is convinced he saw a funnel-web spider.

From 'hell,' we wound our way up a steep, carved stone staircase, where serene, angelic scenes decorated the walls of the cave and into the bright light of 'heaven.' After the bright sunshine, it was weird having to return the same way, through the dark malevolence, to leave. It was something of a relief to visit the 'heaven' cave after that. A large cavern with a natural 'skylight' (a hole in the top of the cave) that allowed the sunlight to shine down on the altars and statues of Buddha. We enjoyed a fun dinner with our new friend Herb that night. It was our last night in DaNang before we moved on to Hoi An. As it turned out, Herb's next destination was also Hoi An, so we swapped numbers and arranged to meet up there for a tour.

From the moment we arrived in Hoi An, I began to feel a sense of impending doom. It was disturbing. News reports suggested that there was a possibility of borders being closed to the whole of SouthEast Asia, or at the very least, requiring quarantine of anyone traveling from the area. I didn't want to be alarmist and leave South East Asia before seeing and doing everything we'd planned, but my senses were tingling and I just knew that I wouldn't be able to spend a whole month there. This feeling was aggravated by the growing number of reports about the Coronavirus being spread to other countries. I called Lainie for advice, and she helped me to make sense of it. But I was still worried. How would Toby cope in Vietnam if I were to get ill? I couldn't ignore my intuition, which was telling me to find another continent. I had started to worry about how to look after him in Thailand when I'd thought my leg might be broken, but somehow, I think we would have coped. Here, I wasn't convinced. It made sense to move to a country further removed from the developing crisis.

In an extreme stretch of comfort zones, I ultimately decided that it was time for us to visit India. I'd never thought I'd ever have the courage to travel to India. It seemed so far, and so different than everything we were familiar with.

Three days and two flights later, with a layover in Kuala Lumpur and 9 hours in the air in total, we arrived in New Delhi. We'd arrived too late for me to get a SIM card for my phone at the airport, so we exited the building without one to see if we could find the Uber that our Airbnb host had arranged. We were standing around, probably looking like exactly what we were: lost tourists. A man approached, and with a sing-song voice asked where we were staying. I said, "South Delhi."

"Oh no, ma'am, you can't go there; there are protests. I'll take you somewhere."

After some debate and a lot of tingling, sensing danger, he let me connect to his phone data so that I could get the number of my host and send him a WhatsApp about our Uber ride. There was no response. He then offered to phone my host; a fast conversation ensued, after which he told me, "Your host isn't there, but the gentleman who answered says there are protests and it'll be better for you to stay at a hotel for a day or two."

He showed me on his phone that he had in fact dialled the number I had for my host. He said he could get me to the tourist board office downtown for 500 Rupees. As I'd already been quoted between 300 and 500 Rupees to get to the Airbnb, I agreed to go with him. He put our luggage into the trunk of a car and opened the doors for Toby and me. Inside the car was another man to whom he gave instructions. I worried all the way there. We didn't know the man who was driving us, and the traffic was frightening, even worse than what we'd experienced in Vietnam. By the time we arrived at the government tourist agency, I was shaking. Neither Toby nor I spoke once during that crazy drive.

The man at the tourist agency, Ifram, spoke good English and was most helpful. "No ma'am, that place is too far, and there are protests." He booked us into a hotel and then invited Toby and me to join him and his family for dinner at their home the next day. He said he had a son Toby's age. Unsure of the man, we politely declined his offer. He also took it on himself to get me a refund for my unused accommodation. He said he had connections who could help with accommodation, because it was a crazy time of the year with Holi celebrations beginning on 9 March.

We stayed two nights at the hotel, where Ifram visited us in the lobby and offered to help us book a tour of India, seeing as Toby and I were both scared, overwhelmed, and exhausted. We'd been warned so many times of scams, and there was no way that I was going to be able to drive us around India. We were grateful for his help, and I paid in full. It wasn't cheap, it meant a significant dip into my savings, but it was a dream come true. Fifty-six days in India, with a private driver to each location, except for the nights when we'd be on overnight trains in 2nd class sleepers. Breakfast was included every day, as well as 3 star hotels, a 6-day yoga retreat, exploring Goa, and various tours.

We moved on to Agra, the home of the famed Taj Mahal, the next day. We'd booked a tour of the Taj Mahal, only to find when we got there that the tours were not included. None of them. We were left to do battle with 'tour guides,' many of whom were operating illegally and charging more than an official guide would. So, at most places, we Googled information ahead of the tours and just walked around by ourselves, ignoring the 'guides' that badgered us at the entrances. Only at the Taj Mahal did we hire a tour guide, and we were happy that we did.

I was annoyed to discover that Ifram hadn't been entirely open and honest about this trip, and started worrying about the fact that I didn't have all the hotel names and contact numbers. A Google search also revealed that I could have bought the same trip for about five thousand Canadian Dollars less! For four nights, I tossed and turned, then in the early hours of the morning, wrote a scathing text to the organizer. Luckily, I first sent it to an old friend Deidre Kostek, who calmed me down and advised against sending it. Instead, she suggested I should talk to our driver who was there with us. I did as she suggested, and a few hours later, received confirmation of all our train tickets and the names of the hotels. This gave me renewed faith in our driver. He was honest. He told me that if he recommended a store or restaurant to us, he'd get a favor in return. This, he told us, was just how India worked. If we ate at a restaurant of his choosing, he'd get a free meal.

'Delhi Belly,' it turned out, was not just a rumor. Maybe because we were on a budget, the food we bought was questionable, or maybe it was just that the bacteria we were exposed to were foreign to our guts. I don't know, but we were lucky that on the occasions when we became ill, it was always evening and in the privacy of our hotel with our own bathroom. The public toilets in India were not what we were accustomed to. Some were simply holes dug into the ground that you squatted over, and others looked like the ones we had at home, but the cleanliness of them was, well, other than in fancy hotels, they just weren't clean at all.

Toby was somewhat of a celebrity in India with his blond hair and Superman cap. Everywhere we went, people stared and asked to take selfies with him. Sometimes, we had to walk away almost rudely after being held up for too long for these picture sessions. Speaking of what we perceive as rude, there didn't appear to be any such thing as a line-up in the places we visited in India. There was an 'every man for himself' mentality that sat uncomfortably with us. Toby especially, because adults thought nothing of shoving kids out of the way if they wanted to get ahead. I had to calm him down a few times when he was manhandled. He spent a lot of time on edge; the constant honking of horns frightened him. I had to explain that it was just a different way of life. It's how traffic goes in India, and there was nothing we could do to change it.

If the traffic wasn't scary enough, just walking in the streets felt like we were taking our lives in our hands. Between trying to avoid cow patties, and the cows themselves, as well as herds of goats that wove between the pedestrians and traffic; we were trying not to be hit by tuk tuks or scooters screaming by with horns blaring, and dealing with hucksters trying to sell us everything from fish to snake oil. The hawkers' street cries added to the audio confusion. Every sense was assaulted in the streets of India.

Having said that, none of this is a criticism of the Indian lifestyle, they are simply observations on how different life is in a country with 1.5 billion people and enormous poverty. Yet, there are many lessons that some western civilizations could learn from them. Their generosity to animals and their fellow humans was incredibly touching. We constantly saw people who had precious little for themselves feeding beggars or giving money to those asking in the streets. We found that generosity was a way of life for them, and part of their religion, whether they were Hindu or Muslim.

On the 25th of February, our driver drove us 6 hours to Jodhpur, a crazy big, loud city. Toby and I headed down the street and settled on a small restaurant for lunch. A few moments later, the restaurant suddenly filled up, leaving only the two extra chairs at our table available. When an English speaking couple came in, I invited them to join us, and was really glad that I did. He was from the UK and she was from Israel. They weren't actually a couple, just friends who'd met during the course of their travels. Both were well traveled, but he had traveled extensively in India. They were charming to talk to, and as a result of watching these two pros in action in the restaurant and on the streets afterwards, my confidence grew.

A 17-hour train ride to Mumbai challenged both Toby's and my mathematical skills. How does it take 17 hours to travel 935 kilometers at 90 kilometers an hour? We also found that the term 'sleeper train' is a misnomer. Neither of us slept a wink. It was impossible with the amount of noise. We were packed tight, and everybody had a mobile phone set to full volume. If it wasn't the phones, it was general conversation, sometimes shouted to mates further down the carriage, or the constant background of hacking coughs. It seemed like at least half of the occupants were sick. Rather alarming given all the Coronavirus coverage in the press.

Stiff and tired, we were met at the station by what we assumed was our driver. As it turned out, he wasn't; he was just there to escort us. He hailed a taxi, then produced his son, who'd arrived on the same train, and the four of us squeezed into one of the tiniest cars I've ever seen. Him up front with the driver, and me, Toby, and the man's son on the back seat. I had to hide my chagrin when crossing the impressive Bandra-Worli Sea Link bridge; I was unable to take a picture due to lack of space in the car.

We were dropped off on the side of a busy street and told to walk down the street for about half a block with our bags; the street was closed due to construction. Toby and I were both out of sorts by now, and trying to escape the vendors that crowded us. As we tried to navigate over construction barriers carrying a backpack, a purse, and both our suitcases, one last man gave it a try, politely saying, "Ma'am, please, come and look at the lovely things I have for you to buy; come, it'll only take a minute."

I snapped. I'm not proud of it, but I was hot, exhausted, and hassled. "Sir!" I exclaimed. "Does it fucking look like I need to buy more stuff? What makes you think a woman carrying this much stuff would be interested in shopping RIGHT NOW?" With that, all of the vendors melted away.

At the hotel, still smarting from the last 20 hours, we discovered that due to Holi, and changes in train schedules, our tours in Mumbai and Goa were cancelled. Our 'agent' couldn't book alternate trains, so we would have a driver for the rest of the trip. While this meant less train time than initially planned, it also meant additional stops in locations not on the original schedule and hotels I would have to pay for.

On the plus side, the Gateway of India, an arched monument built to commemorate the visit of King George V and Queen Mary in 1911, was less than a block from our hotel, which meant that we could access tourist attractions without paying for a cab. The following morning, refreshed and mood restored after a good night's sleep, Toby and I visited the monument, then walked to a market via a slum (that bit was unplanned). We had been keen to eat at a famous eatery called Leopold Café; we had been warned that it was pricey, but worth it for the atmosphere and history. But, on opening the menu, we had to change our plans, atmosphere and history would have to wait. The same dish we'd paid between 150 and 200 Rupees for in other parts of India was listed for 700 Rupees.

We ended up at McDonalds. An odd choice, I know, but we were hungry and it was nearby. There we met a woman from New York City whose husband worked in Mumbai from time to time. She suggested that we visit the hanging gardens and the Old Woman's Shoe. She explained that cabs were fine to take in Mumbai because they all had working meters and were trustworthy. She told me how much to pay the cabbie, and not to accept a higher price. She also said that if anyone tried to rip us off, there were always police at the taxi ranks that we could report them to. Feeling much more confident, that's just what we did; we took a stroll in the hanging gardens and park where the Old Woman's Shoe was, then on down to the beach to enjoy the sunset. As luck would have it, we found ourselves near a very nice little restaurant where we could enjoy dinner before taking a cab back to the hotel.

The next day we took a ferry to Elephanta Island, an island with a series of carved temples dedicated to the god Shiva. We met an Australian couple there who had paid a guide for a private tour of the island, and they asked him if we could tag along. He very good naturedly agreed, so we had a free tour of the island. We were happy to contribute by giving him a tip on behalf of the group; he'd been incredibly informative. Leanne, the Australian lady, was a wonderful generous soul, we swapped numbers, and have maintained contact ever since. Our circle of friends was growing, and becoming quite diverse.

I had expected India to be different, but was still amazed by some of these differences. Smog was a serious issue in Mumbai. If we woke early enough in the morning, we could actually watch it rolling in over the city. One day traveling on the equivalent of an interstate highway, we saw a man lying on his back, with his arms folded across his chest mummy-style in the shade of his big truck, pulled over on the side of the road. When I suggested to our driver that we stop and help him, as I thought he was working on a repair job, the driver laughed. "No, ma'am, he's just sleeping."

Traffic jams were multiple daily occurrences. What was particularly unusual about these traffic jams, though, was that they were, more often than not, caused by animals. We experienced traffic jams caused by cows, camels, goats, sleeping dogs, sheep, and even dogs chasing wild pigs in the streets. The scooter, we discovered, was far more widely and ingeniously used in India than anywhere else we'd been. The maximum number of people we saw on one scooter was five! We also saw two grown men and two goats on one scooter. Probably our most fascinating scooter sighting was that of a scooter towing a cow loaded into a wheelbarrow-like contraption. Toby and I were both fascinated, amused, and appalled. We could just imagine the Canadian police's response to some of these scenarios. Scooter usage would need to be a whole extra subject in their training.

On a walk in Mumbai, we managed once again, despite having Google Maps (or maybe because of it!) to get lost. This was an eye-opener. Near the hanging gardens, we'd marvelled at the huge mansions that people lived in—properties worth in excess of a million US dollars. Now, off the beaten track, we stumbled upon the slums of India. Strangely, we felt safer there than we did in the city. The residents didn't bother us in the least; they just stared in surprise at these tourists in their space. For Toby and me, though, it really drove home the huge differences in social standing and wealth for the people of India. We left the slums feeling emotionally shaken. We'd never seen so many people living in such cramped quarters. The slum was huge, but tiny by comparison to the number of dwellers. We couldn't help but speculate as to the devastating outcome if a virus like the Coronavirus topping all the news headlines at the time should ever reach this area. Social distancing was a physical impossibility.

Our second long train ride was from Mumbai to Goa. It was every bit as uncomfortable as the first. My shoulder was already sore from the previous 17-hour trip, I'm a side sleeper, and just can't fall asleep any other way. Our bunk mate, an older lady, was very ill, coughing and sniffling continually. Her hand kept going to her forehead and she sweated profusely. I couldn't help worrying about the pandemic that was now spreading further afield, and eventually, took Toby and our luggage and went in search of another bunk. Fortunately, the train was not full and we were able to find another carriage that could accommodate us. We arrived in Goa at 5:45 a.m., tired and stressed.

My mood ratcheted down a few more notches when there was no sign of our promised driver. Standing on the platform next to our luggage, I texted Ifram, who responded ten minutes later that he couldn't get a hold of the driver and we should catch a cab. He'd reimburse me. I was upset, suspicious, and not holding out much hope for the reimbursement. We found a cab, and 1500 Rupees later (about $30 CAD), we arrived at the hotel where we were told that our room would only be ready at 2 p.m. Another call to Ifram revealed that he was just as out of sorts, and he wasn't willing to deal with the issue outside of regular office hours. Toby and I curled up on the couches in the lobby, each with a hand through the straps of our bags. We were woken by hotel staff at 10:30 a.m., and ushered to our rooms, where a soft king-sized bed and air conditioning awaited.

We couldn't sleep all day, though. We had an interesting mission to accomplish in a strange place. Before we'd left Canada, we'd had our first two Twinrix shots, a vaccine against

Hepatitis A and B, but with two shots, your protection would last about a year. In order to extend that protection to a lifetime, it was necessary to have a third shot six months after the first two. Our six months were nearly up. The hotel concierge suggested that we go to the pharmacy. At the pharmacy, we were told to go to the hospital. At the hospital, we were told to go back to the pharmacy, purchase the shots, and return to the hospital to have them administered. Back at the pharmacy, we were told "wrong pharmacy." Wearily, we walked two kilometers, in the blazing heat, in search of the next one on the other side of town.

We never found the other pharmacy, but we did find another hospital. At the emergency room, there were two nurses, multi-tasking like I've never seen before. There didn't seem to be any order at all. No line-up, no paperwork; they were both answering questions, giving injections, and putting Band-Aids on kids, all at the same time. We watched this for a while, waiting our turn, but eventually realizing that 'turns' didn't exist, I just joined the fray, projecting my voice and stating our case. "Ok, ok. Five minutes, you see doctor. Sit, sit." The nurse pointed out the door, where found chairs. Half an hour later, we were still sitting there in the passage outside the emergency room. Eventually, I got up and stuck my head back in the door. The nurse looked up from her patient. "Oh, oh. I forget. One moment." She took our yellow vaccine cards and disappeared through a door, then emerged a few moments later. "Doctor says it's ok. Sit, sit."

Five minutes later, the nurse was back with us, explaining that they didn't have Twinrix, but they did have separate Hepatitis A and Hepatitis B shots that were essentially the same thing, just two separate injections. Neither of us had issues with needles, so agreed that we would take the two shots offered instead. "Ok, ok," she said, "but we only have one Hep A and

2 Hep Bs, so you come back tomorrow for other Hep A." Really worn out now, I asked if they could order the other Hepatitis A shot, and we'd return the next day to do all the shots in one go.

The following day, the nurse recognized us immediately and said, "You need to see Doctor first." She ushered us into a hot, humid office, where the doctor was seated behind his desk. There were already four other patients in there at the same time, so now, with us and the nurse, we were seven. The nurse spoke quickly in Hindi.

The doctor pointed to Toby, and said, "How old?"

"I'm eleven."

"Good." The doctor nodded. "Full shot."

We were ushered out again, and the nurse administered the shots (and yes, I checked that the needles were brand new and removed from their wrapping in front of us). The nurse took our vaccine cards to the doctor for signing, then we stepped up to the counter to pay. I was surprised to find that there was no charge for the nurses or the doctor. All we had to pay was for the four injections, which came to 3,500 Rupees (about $64.88 at that day's exchange rate). I'd expected it to be much more, given we'd paid $320 CAD back home.

Our vaccination issues took up most of the time we had in Goa; the following day, we enjoyed one day at the beach before packing up for the drive to Alleppy. Here we were able to wind down the pace a bit. We were booked for a 24-hour houseboat cruise on the canals. It was humid and over 37 degrees Celsius as we floated down the canals surrounded by rice paddies. We had the boat to ourselves, just us, the captain, and the cook. We lounged beneath a woven canopy, appreciative of the light breeze, enjoying watching locals fishing and interacting. We stopped at a fisherman's house, where we bought the most enormous freshwater shrimp either of us had ever seen for our dinner. Six shrimp weighed a whole kilogram, and we only paid 450 Rupees for them (about $8).

That evening, the captain docked at the shore for the night, and the peace of the day was shattered. The shrimp were heavenly, but that was the only highlight of the night. Mosquitos descended in clouds, and the locals partied on both shores, with music louder than I'd ever heard in my night-clubbing days. What made it worse was that it was two completely different styles of Indian music, which clashed in my brain. Along the shores, each party had lit huge smoky bonfires to keep the mosquitos at bay. Our eyes burned from the smoke, and our lungs coughed in protest. We doused ourselves in Citronella oil, and took our Malaria pills.

The following day, our boat returned us to our starting point, gently, and we were once again at peace with the world. From there we were driven to an Ayurvedic and Yoga retreat where we were going to enjoy being pampered, and taking care of our holistic health. It wasn't to be. On arrival, we were greeted with the news that India would be closing its borders in the next couple of days in response to the spreading Coronavirus pandemic. I spent two days on the phone, trying to work out where to go next, then at the last moment, called our driver to come and get us. He drove us directly to the nearest airport, which was ghostly quiet and stressed, everyone in masks. From there we flew to Chennai, where people still thronged, not a mask in sight. There, I tried to change our flight out of India before all flights stopped. I was shocked to discover that the insurance agent had forgotten to tick a box on a form, rendering our cancellation insurance null and void.

I called Ifram to cancel the second month of our two-month tour of India. He informed me that there would be no refund, insisting that every penny I'd paid him had been spent. I was angry and tearful, but didn't have time to either fight or indulge in hysterics. We needed to leave India before it locked down. It took four days, hundreds of calls, pleading and begging, and a huge chunk of my savings to get us out of India. We eventually flew out from Chennai to London the day before India halted all flights in and out of the country, and the government announced that it wouldn't even be repatriating their own citizens.

Chapter 13:

Regrouping and Moving On

From a practical perspective, it was a relief to be back in the English speaking world after six months of traveling in countries where English was not widely spoken. It was easier to discuss issues and plan our way forward. On the down side, the cost of accommodation, meals, well—everything, was really high. My bank account had taken a huge hit just getting us out of India. Not only were we now not able to use the money spent on our next month's accommodations, but we were having to support ourselves on a weaker currency. Any treats were out of the question.

Psychologically, I was on the verge of a nervous breakdown, having had to fight to get a flight out of India, fight for refunds (of which none were forthcoming), plan accommodation (which changed almost daily) dealing with the constantly changing flights that we were waitlisted for, all the while ensuring that we ate and had somewhere to sleep while packing up and moving on. I was sleep deprived and stressed. Throughout our journey, I'd even noticed that my PTSD and post concussive symptoms had reduced to the point that they were almost negligible, but in the midst of the pandemic panic, they returned in full force. I became scatterbrained and completely lost the ability to multitask in any manner. Toby was frustrated too, because according to him, I hadn't completed a sentence in two days. I'd start to say something and then just fade off.

The plan in flying to the UK was that, from there, it would be easy to access almost any European destination. We were considering Brussels as our next stop. At Gatwick airport, despite some flight restrictions, it had been business as usual. We weren't advised to self isolate, so we bought bus tickets and headed for our Airbnb. It was quite strange understanding everyone around us, and them understanding us. We'd gotten used to being able to hold our own conversations freely, knowing that others around us didn't understand. Our hostess was amazing, and her attic room was large and comfortable with soft warm beds and plenty of duvets. The comfort was a treat all on its own.

Within hours of arriving in the UK, the call had been put out by the Canadian government for Canadians to return home; we were able to book a ticket, but only in eight days' time. We headed into central London on our first full day, and did some rather sketchy grocery shopping. The shops were largely devoid of supplies, food, and people. We took a long walk from Victoria Station, past Buckingham Palace and Westminster Abbey. The sites were closed, and the city was quiet, so we just took photographs from a distance. We had a picnic, then continued on foot to the Tower of London, which was open. Unnerved by all the media reports, and not sure whether it would be possible to maintain safe distances, we decided not to go in for a tour.

I'd made a call to the Canadian Embassy earlier in the morning to see if we could move our flight earlier; they called back that afternoon and said no. At least we had a flight, and they needed to focus their resources on those that didn't. By the end of our long walk, we were tired, and it appeared the world had changed again. News was that London was being shut down and people were told to self isolate and be prepared for the long haul. Returning to our neighborhood near Gatwick, the stores were empty, people were avoiding each other on the streets, and there were long line-ups at the pharmacies.

For the next two days, Toby and I holed up in our attic apartment watching the news, and the ever-increasing statistics. Suddenly, I couldn't sit there waiting anymore. We packed up our things and headed for the airport with the intention of staying there until we could get a flight out. That same morning, there was an Air Transat flight out, and although it had been overbooked, many passengers hadn't shown up by the check in deadline of 45 minutes pre-flight. Not only did Toby and I both get seats on that flight, but they were two seats together! I cried while we were clearing security, then pulled myself together and we rushed to get on the plane. Once seated, I cried again. Somewhere over the Atlantic, I bawled. Toby just looked perplexed and kept squeezing my hand, telling me it was all going to be fine. I couldn't even explain to him why I was crying. After that last bawling session, I calmed down. We were headed home in the middle of a worldwide pandemic and our angels were with us, likely sighing a huge sigh of relief.

To be honest, I'm not sure that there was any single event or person that prompted all the emotion. I guess it was a number of things. Some of which were conflicting. I was devastated that our world travel plans had come to an end, but relieved that if the worst was going to happen, it was going to happen at home and not in India. I was tired, angry, sad, and pretty much broke. I was scared, for me, for Toby, for my parents, and yes, for everyone in the world. I was scared for the people in the slums of India who had no chance of isolating or social distancing. I was angry with Ifram, for overcharging me and refusing to refund me, and I was angry with the universe for throwing a virus at the world just six months after we'd scraped together the courage and budget to explore it. I was angry for Toby who was missing out on a promised education with a difference. But most of all, I was scared for our future. I was scared of returning to 'normal,' of giving up our hopes and dreams. I imagine it's akin to how a caged bird feels when it's escaped, soaring above the garden, only to be hunted by an eagle and having to dodge the eagle's talons, retreating to the safety of its cage again. It was bittersweet.

Landing in Toronto, I felt equal measures of both relief and failure. I texted Kevin, who had at the last minute arranged to fetch us. He let us know where to find him in the parking area outside. It was strange to arrive at an empty arrivals hall, but the pandemic had changed everything. When I saw my Kevin, smiling and waving from his truck, the relief outweighed the sense of failure. Despite our break up, we had managed to hold on to our friendship, and it was nice to catch up on the way home. Our house was still rented out for the next six months, but fortunately, Toby and I were able to move into the basement apartment, which was available.

Talking about cages, it was a strange new Canada that we returned to. We were confined to the basement for a 14-day quarantine period. After constantly packing and moving and experiencing new things, this was difficult. Toby and I took drives just for a change in scenery; we had enough fuel to not have to stop and interact with others. We also took long walks in the evenings when all our neighbors went inside for dinner. It had a new name now; it wasn't just a generic coronavirus. It was Covid-19. For 14 days, we didn't go to the shops or see other people. Friends very kindly ran errands for us and kept us in groceries, or I ordered goods online, which were delivered to the back deck without human contact. Frustrated by being cooped up, I implemented a yoga hour. After the first one, Toby suggested that half an hour was plenty, so we compromised and made it 45 minutes. With so much free time on our hands, I also started sorting through memories to write a book. This book.

Once our isolation period was over and we were free to go shopping, it held little appeal; all that was open were the grocery stores. Toby, not usually a fan of grocery shopping, even volunteered to accompany me just to escape. It was a mission to mask up and shop, sanitizing at each stop, then sanitizing ourselves and our groceries on our return. It wasn't the outing we'd thought it would be. So, we resigned ourselves to waiting out this virus at home. The news on television was depressing. Statistics worldwide were alarming. People were angry and pointing fingers at each other. Even governments were pointing fingers at other countries, and blaming their own citizens. Everybody seemed to be looking for someone to blame. I could feel the anger, and I took it on. I became angry. When friends proudly told me of how they'd broken curfew, or snuck out to visit with each other, I got angry. I just wanted everyone to bunker down and be good. I felt sure that if we could get that right, this thing would go away. It would die out, for lack of host bodies. I felt that the longer people 'played' with rules, the longer they broke the rules and thought those rules only applied to everyone else because they were in some way special, the longer lockdown would last for everyone. I wanted this to be over so that I could enjoy the great outdoors in July and August.

As April turned into May, and May into June, I started to realize that Covid-19 was unlikely to be leaving anytime soon. Hopes for herd immunity were dwindling. Many of us had cherished hopes that antibodies would build up and Covid-19 would become no more threatening than the common cold. We all needed to accept that it was going to be around for a long time to come, and we needed to learn how to live with it, instead of waiting for it to go away.

Slowly, we started venturing out in our 'bubbles' and started living our 'new normal.' I spent some time in self-reflection, contemplating the next phase of my life. I felt inspired by our travels and by my own growth both spiritual and in confidence. I'd moved beyond my comfort zone, flexed my wings, and tested my abilities. Successfully curing Toby of air sickness through hypnosis had helped me to appreciate my own skills. It was time for me to put more focus on my online business, Intuitive Butterfly. While I'd previously done dozens of courses, and was by no means lacking in qualifications, I'd allowed others to plant doubts in my mind. I no longer did. I knew that I was fortunate to have the skills and gifts that I had, and I could no longer hide them in shame, or fear of embarrassing or angering skeptics. I was as entitled to my opinions and peace in my life as the skeptics were.

There was enough space and diversity in the world for everyone. There will always be duality. There will always be haves and have-nots. There will always be abusers and victims; there will always be pragmatists and spiritualists. There will always be room for improvement. Every government, good or bad, will continue to have an opposition, and every religion its supporters and detractors. But as long as there's a measure of tolerance, patience, and kindness, there will be a way to find common ground and understanding. My mission in life is not to impress those who don't understand me—nor to convert them. It's not to impress anyone. Least of all those whose beliefs are diametrically opposite to mine. It's to be true to myself, and to help, guide, and teach where I can, and where it's wanted.

I've always been mouthy and opinionated, and let's get this straight, that hasn't changed that much. I will probably still go to battle over issues. I like to think, though, that I am better at choosing my battles and walking away from those that are not worth the pain. I started looking forward to the future, to helping steer Toby through the minefields that had plagued my fifty years of life, and prevented me from liking myself, or even getting to know myself. What a terrible waste of time. If Toby could learn to know himself, like himself, and be comfortable in his own skin from a young age, that time wouldn't have been wasted. It would have been a valuable lesson. Suddenly, things were falling into place. Making sense.

For some, success is measured in dollars, or material goods. For others, it is measured in quality of life, or happiness. I needed to strive for what made us happy, and nobody else was qualified to judge my success. This didn't make me selfish. As a mother, my success would also be measured by Toby's happiness. He is my first priority in life, and always will be. If there was a 'Mother-of-the-Year-Award,' I probably wouldn't even qualify to enter, but if one day I have the pleasure of having a well-rounded, confident, intelligent, kind, caring, and unfettered adult son, that will be my satisfaction. Already, I believe that he is more comfortable in his own skin at twelve than I was at 24.

In September 2020, the lease on my house was up. It was decision time. Reclaim our home, move back upstairs, and wait and see what changes there would be in the world, or move on. Toby and I discussed our options. International travel was not an option due to all the restrictions, but we both agreed that a digital nomad lifestyle was more appealing than any of the alternatives we could come up with. So was the thought of escaping the Canadian winter. It was time to move on. We decided that three and a half months in Mexico would provide us with the opportunity to learn Spanish.

In the meantime, Toby's education continued, using YouTube and Google, and we took the opportunity of being back in Canada to focus on local history, geography, and culture. He was delighted to be able to take up Tae-kwon-do again, and in November 2020, my heart swelled when he was awarded his black belt. My little man was growing up in so many ways. He was 12 years old and more self-assured and independent than most of his peers.

After some discussion with Toby, I listed the house for sale, and we started on packing up all our possessions, but then I got cold feet and withdrew the listing. A friend of mine was going through a divorce and needed somewhere to stay, so we agreed that he could stay in the house, shovel the drive, and generally look after things while his divorce went through and we followed our hearts to Mexico. The plan was that by the time we returned in March, his affairs would be settled and we could move back into the house for our 14-day quarantine, during which time we'd list the house for sale and pack it up. The best time to list a house in Canada is usually around April. We wanted to use some of the capital to buy another fifth-wheel trailer and truck that we could use to tour Canada in the summer while we waited for international borders to reopen. When that happened, we hoped to ship the rig across the Panama Canal and into South America for 2022. Being able to speak Spanish would allow us to explore further afield than the tourist routes.

We eventually flew to Mexico on the 13th of December, arriving in Puerto Vallarta a little later than originally anticipated due to frozen lines on the plane in Calgary. It had been minus 17 degrees Celsius when we left. Our Airbnb was small, but cute-small rather than cramped-small. It was functional and comfortable and very conveniently located, just a half hour's walk to the beach, with a Costco and another supermercado within walking distance. The following day, we were on the beach in our swimsuits, revelling in the warm weather.

Later that day, we were joined by Lainie Liberti, the moderator of the We Are World Schoolers Facebook group, and the organizer of the summit we'd attended in Spain. Her flight was also delayed—this time by five hours. It was wonderful to catch up and be able to pick her brain. She had a huge amount of travel knowledge and experience working with teens. She ran a very successful teen mentor program, and will no doubt be a guiding hand in Toby's and my lives as we head into the unknown teenage parenting years.

We spent a wonderful week of 'winter vacation' in Puerto Vallarta, enjoying the stunning beaches, and the cleverly made sand sculptures of Banderas Bay. Toby was fascinated by the colorful iguanas that looked like mini dragons; one particularly spiky fellow with an orange crest lived in the tree outside our window and became Toby's unofficial non-house pet. Puerto Vallarta is a popular winter holiday destination, and they pulled out all the stops to keep the tourists entertained. Mariachi music was played in the open, *Danza de los Voladores,* or the Dance of the Flyers, was an acrobatic show on top of a long pole that took place on the Malecon promenade. There were also free shows at the Los Arcos Amphitheater with lots of dancing and singing, plenty of street food, of course, and artisanal markets.

We also did another fear-facing zipline. That would have been a costly exercise, but an opportunity presented itself to do it for free, if I was willing to sit through a timeshare presentation.

There was plenty of time in my budget, just not a whole lot of money, so I was willing to sacrifice the time for the fun. Actually, the timeshare resort looked pretty good, but at an annual fee of $1,500 for a week of holiday, was definitely out of our league; that was almost a month's budget.

After a whole week of hedonistic fun in the sun, it was time to take the business of education more seriously, and we settled into a small two-bedroom apartment in Guanajuato. It was really comfortable, and we'd taken a three-month lease instead of booking Airbnbs, in the interests of our dwindling finances. It not only had two bedrooms, it had two bathrooms too, and a lovely rooftop terrace where we could enjoy the sunset and the sights and sounds of the neighborhood. Lainie was also staying in Guanajuato, about 15 minutes walk from our apartment, and spent a few days showing us around.

We had a quiet Christmas day, Lainie took us for a walk, helped us find our bearings, and treated us to the most sinful decadence: a cup of warm freshly melted semi-sweet chocolate served in a teacup. We bought a roasted chicken from a barbecue vendor on the side of the road, which was delicious, and had plenty of leftovers to make tacos with afterwards. Christmas night was not so quiet as we discovered that the Mexicans party like mad, and lying in bed, we were entertained by fireworks and music until four o' clock in the morning. Only to be woken by church bells at 5 a.m.

A couple of days later, a cold snap had us shivering. I dug around in a closet and found an old propane heater, which I set up in my bedroom to take the chill out of the air while Toby and I brushed our teeth and got ready for bed. I pulled the bedroom door closed behind me to trap in the toasty air. The door made a funny double clicking sound as it closed, and I turned the latch to check it only to find it locked.

I immediately imagined the unattended propane heater in my now locked room bursting into flames, and the whole building catching alight. I dashed downstairs and grabbed the one and only bunch of keys. Not one worked. My next thought was to phone our landlord's assistant, who I'd been told lived nearby, but we weren't sure exactly where. Nope. My phone was also locked in the room. I ran back downstairs and threw open the front door; there must have been about 50 nighttime revellers passing by. I called out to them (in English) trying to ask if I could borrow a phone. I wasn't sure if they were just ignoring me, or trying to avoid this crazy gringo yelling out into the streets in her pyjamas. Judging by their facial expressions, I'd guess the latter.

Toby grabbed a scrap of paper off the kitchen counter with Kelly's (the landlord's assistant) phone number on it, and ran to a local corner *tienda* (store) to see if they would allow him to make a call. They were closed. He ran back, panting from his exertion. "Mom, the shop's closed, but there's a guy who said I could use his phone. But the number isn't working."

"Remember it's a local call; you've got to leave off the international dial code."

"Oh duh!" he yelled, slapping himself on the forehead and skidding back around the corner.

He was back in minutes. "Kelly's coming."

While we waited, I tried my hand at lock picking without luck. Then, falling back on something I'd seen in a movie, I took a business card and wiggled it between the door and the frame. Murphy's law, just as Kelly arrived at the front door, the bedroom door popped open. I was mortified at all the consternation we'd caused, but relieved to see that there was no smoke billowing out from the bedroom; everything was calm and the propane heater burned gently.

The following day, Toby and I went out and purchased an electric heater.

Guanajuato is about 1990 meters above sea level, and surrounded by hills and mountains. From our apartment to our favorite grocery store is a steep climb to almost 2200 meters. Lots of exercise for Toby and me. The hills are steep and the roads incredibly narrow. We quickly learned to walk up the hill to the store, and then catch a cab down with our bags. The first time we did this, on getting into the cab, I noticed that every light on the dashboard shone like a Christmas tree; this didn't inspire much confidence. I gave the driver our address, and he shrugged and nodded. Not the most talkative chap, or maybe it was the language barrier. The sooner we learned to converse in Spanish, the better.

As we reached the summit, it felt like a precipice leading down to our home. He braked sharply at the entrance to the narrow winding descent, stopped the car, made a sign of the cross, took a deep breath, and eased the car forward. It felt like a carnival ride that tests your nerve. I was holding on tight all the way, my feet firmly planted on the ground as if I was braking. Toby and I stared at each other wide-eyed. Fortunately, the brakes did seem to be working, and we made it in one piece.

We soon fell into an easy routine of sleeping late, attending an hour's Spanish class at a school nearby, then exploring the area. We ate cheaply; our dinners consisted largely of guacamole and corn tortilla chips, spaghetti, and soups with bakery buns made into garlic bread, and egg sandwiches, which we packed for lunches. At least twice a week we tried different street foods, either for lunch or for dinner. This was sometimes hilarious as we attempted to find the less spicy foods, oftentimes unsuccessfully in the beginning. We soon discovered that the best remedy to the chili problem, when our ordering went awry, was a rice water and cinnamon drink, Horchata. Once again, one of the first things we had to learn was how to request non-spicy dishes: no picante!

After our Spanish lessons, we explored Guanajuato largely on foot. We were delighted to discover that it is home to a number of museums and art galleries. Unfortunately, almost all of them were closed due to Covid. The only one that was open, we visited a couple of times. It was a bit on the creepy side. The Museo de las Momias de Guanajuato; otherwise fondly referred to as the Museum of the Mummies. What made it particularly macabre was the realization that we were looking at actual dead bodies. Many of them had died of cholera in the 1800s and been buried immediately; there were even suggestions that some might have been inaccurately declared dead, or buried during the last throes of their illness. I could believe this, seeing the expressions of torment on some of their faces. One mummy was from my own lifetime, buried in 1965 and exhumed in 1973, I felt chilled by the reality that this brought home to me. Every single one of those mummies had been a living, breathing, laughing, loving human being, as ordinary as you or me. Life is so temporary and fragile, with no guarantees.

We were particularly sad that the Centro de Ciencias Explora, or the Science Museum, was closed. Toby has a science book that I ordered online for him, which is quite dogeared and goes just about everywhere we do, and this would have been the perfect place for him. We'd researched it online, and it appeared that it was interactive and incredibly educational. It houses everything from ancient locomotives and aircraft to a planetarium and vivarium. Entry was also free, so we could have visited as often as we liked. But, no, thanks to the pandemic paranoia, we were stymied.

I received a number of texts from my friend who was looking after our house during this time, but in January, these started to take on a different tone, familiar and almost 'boyfriend-like.' I was uncomfortable, but not too stressed, as he was far away and there wasn't any chance of him getting ideas about a potential relationship. I kept my texts firmly in the 'friend zone' and tried to ignore the feeling in my gut that something wasn't right. In January, when further lockdowns were being touted, I got an angry message from him, insisting that we would be stupid to get locked down in Mexico, and demanding that we return home immediately. I responded that we had no intention of changing our plans. His response, "Just remember that if you can't come back, tenants have all the rights."

Was he kidding? My antennae were up, and I was foreseeing trouble. I couldn't afford to take any chances. The one thing I could not afford to do was lose my house, my biggest (financial) asset. I immediately called my real estate agent, Ray, and asked him to list the house for sale again. I held out little hope that the house would sell, not in January, and certainly not in the middle of a pandemic. The house went up for sale at about two o'clock on a Wednesday afternoon. By 8 p.m. that night, it had been shown three times, and by 9 p.m., another four showings had been booked for the following day. By Friday morning, the house was sold.

Who'd have thought? There were so few houses for sale at that time, due to the pandemic, that demand was high, and fear of price hikes in spring made buyers twitchy. I was shocked. The sale closed quickly, and while I was dealing with the paperwork, I kept checking with Toby. "Are you absolutely sure that you want to carry on living a nomadic lifestyle?"

He was adamant. "I'm sure, Mom. Who wouldn't want to travel full-time?" Whatever gypsy blood made me restless clearly also flowed in his veins

I texted my friend/tenant, which started an avalanche of angry texts about eviction during a pandemic. I remained firm. I explained that his threat of claiming occupation rights to my home had precipitated the sale, and he needed to own that. I also reminded him that as he wasn't paying rent, and didn't have a contract, it wasn't strictly speaking an eviction. Eventually, Ray had to go and ask him nicely to leave. I lost a friend, and our house was sold, but at least it wasn't stolen.

I called my parents and told them of this turn of events. "I think I'm going to have to come home and finish packing up the house," I told my Mom.

"No, Marnie. Between me, Dad, and Ray, we can handle things. Don't stress," she replied. I think they probably lived to regret that offer. It was a far bigger job than they'd anticipated, and while I was relieved not to have to go back, I felt terribly sorry for them tackling such an arduous task at their age. As much as my parents and I have had a bumpy relationship due to our different beliefs and lifestyles, I have to take my hat off to them. When the chips were down, they were always there for me. They have taken on some enormous tasks on my behalf, easing my burden in practical ways. Such is their love. Everybody has different ways of expressing it, and looking back, I now recognize thousands of examples of their love in my life. When I thought I was being neglected, it was because they were working hard to provide for me. As an empath, I'd craved a more physical and emotional love and often overlooked their efforts as just things that parents have to do for their children, rather than the labors of love that they were.

Epilogue

As I write this, the world continues to change and deal with the Covid-19 pandemic, and Toby and I are still in Mexico. Most of the book was written while in quarantine and Gunajuato, but we are currently in stunningly beautiful Puerto Escondido, enjoying a bit of a vacation.

What started out as a virus in China has become a world virus. Governments around the globe have taken severe steps to curb the spread, and many industries, notably travel and hospitality, have suffered badly. Businesses have folded worldwide, and people have been left jobless.

It's hard to work out what's true and what's not in the media frenzy. There is so much fake news. Prime Minister Trudeau, in Canada, has shut down airlines and borders, officially precluding Toby and I from returning for the foreseeable future. While ex-president Donald Trump in the USA faces an impeachment hearing and continues to oppose the wearing of face masks. I can't help but feel that a virus that has a mortality rate of less than 1% has caused far more trouble than it should have. I know this is controversial, because so many people have died. But as I understand it, many more people have died of Malaria and Tuberculosis in the world, and those statistics don't even make mainstream news. Has it been a case of an extreme global overreaction?

Vaccines are being rolled out across the world, at great cost, and amidst enormous suspicion. The virus is mutating, rendering previously successfully tested vaccines less effective. Pro-vaxxers and anti-vaxxers are at loggerheads. One lot touting the vaccine as the solution to world problems, the other lot insisting it's all a big money making scam concocted by big pharmaceutical companies, and a ploy for governments to snatch control from the people. Statistics are unreliable, as in many countries all deaths are recorded as Covid-19 related deaths if blood samples show Covid-19 antibodies. Families are being torn apart by these arguments, both sides seeing the situation as a matter of life and death.

Our greatest fear is the potential introduction of Covid-Vaxx passports. If these should be implemented worldwide, it could have a serious impact on our travel plans.

Is this a deathly plague, or is it just yet another version of the flu? Only time will tell, I guess. But the world is taking it seriously, and I am smelling a rat.

We are not worried about not being able to return to Canada right now; our sights are still set on further travel, but will we be able to travel? Who knows? There is so much uncertainty. We've learned an enormous amount of Spanish grammar, but our vocabularies are nowhere where we need them to be in order to travel widely in South America. Toby is a bit shy about speaking Spanish, and I'm frustrated by my inability to express myself clearly. We still have so much to learn.

It has crossed my mind to return to Canada and wait out this situation, but if we did return now, and if one of us tested positive, we would be forced to isolate in an institution of the government's choosing, at our own expense. It also seems that there would be no guarantee that we would be allowed to stay together. Horror stories of families and couples split by 'Covid regulations' either intentionally or in error are my worst nightmare. Toby and I are a unit, a team.

We are truly grateful for the wonder of the Internet that allows me to work from anywhere, and Toby to learn. He has recently registered for Outschool.com's four-day course on "Fantastic Fails in Science and History." I wonder whether someday in the future, the Covid pandemic will feature in history books as a failure or a win for mankind.

Intuitive Butterfly continues to grow, and my goal is that it will eventually be our main source of income. I derive enormous pleasure in helping others to find clarity in their decision making, and healing for their souls. Life is complicated, and even as a psychic with strong intuition, there have been times in my life that I have needed guidance from others, from people who are able to see beyond the obvious. In particular, objective direction from those who are not impacted by my decisions, who have no vested interest in the choices that I make, but who are able to help me to find my own truth, to reach my own decisions by tapping into my subconscious. There is a wealth of helpful information, emotions, and fears buried in the subconscious that so many people are unable to access. I don't tell people what to do, I help them access this treasure trove of knowledge that gives them the tools to make the best decisions for them.

Toby and I have had a lot of time, and a lot of need, to reflect on life lately. He loves this informal method of schooling, and is learning an enormous amount. If he should ever wish to go to university, the option, in Canada, is still fortunately available to him. As a progressive country, homeschooling is not eschewed, and he would only need to provide reasonable proof of his learning. We are collecting scrapbooks full of receipts from world museums, online courses, and science camps as part of his portfolio, in case he ever decides that he'd like to take that route.

At this stage, he is more interested in learning a trade than following an academic path, but we are both keeping our minds open. So much can change in the intervening years. Lots of people that I know are in completely different career fields to their original field of study. Many people, and here I speak from personal experience, don't know what they want to do, and change direction frequently until much later in life.

I have been a flight attendant, a truck driver, and a property manager. I have a university degree in intuitive counselling, and another in French. I also have a certificate in holistic healing from Seneca College, and more than twenty certificates in more alternative fields, such as hypnotherapy, past life regression, Reiki, and mediumship. But I had never had the courage to be me. All my life, I've sought approval in more conventional fields. I have repressed my natural gifts, learned skills, and passions, because I thought that was what was expected of me.

It's taken me fifty years to acknowledge my own issues, and the only reason that I've managed to do that was because I left my comfort zone. I allowed myself to be stretched, to be challenged. It took the removal of my safety nets for me to recognize that self-sabotage held me back. I would blame others for not supporting me in my interests, but actually, I clung to guilt and toxic relationships because, painful as they were, at least they were familiar. I had to learn to let go.

My first introduction to alternative healing happened 26 years ago. Shortly after my divorce, I was suffering extreme depression, and signed up for an exercise class. It was a new form of movement called Nia, combining jazz, ballet, yoga, and meditation. At the end of the first class, I fled to my car and cried for a good half hour. It was horrible and painful, a deep-seated grief. What followed was a feeling of lightness and relief.

The following week, I had a similar experience, not as long as the first one, but just as intense. I buried my face in my arms on the steering wheel, embarrassed by my tears. The next week, I didn't want to go back. I didn't want to feel or experience that pain ever again. Obviously, though, some part of me did, because I went back for more. I arrived early that week so that I could talk to the teacher, Caroline, about my concerns.

When I told her, she looked delighted. "Marnie, this is great, it means the class is working for you!"

I was confused. "You mean this is supposed to make me cry?"

Her smile was broad. "The whole purpose of this class is to help you get back in touch with yourself, to release the past and that which no longer serves you. We store negative emotions in our bodies that need to be released. If we don't release them, they fester and hold us back."

I was fascinated, and she booked an energy healing session for me with her. It did me a world of good, and I continued under her guidance to read books and do courses. I think in my subconscious, I knew that this was my future, because I continued to study in this line for years. Yet I kept telling myself that despite all these experiences and qualifications, I was an impostor. I didn't have the courage to do things that would embarrass my family. I limited myself, and projected my fears onto them. At the World School Family Summit in October 2019, I caught myself imposing similar restrictions on Toby. It's a behavior that we learn from society. There was a talent show, which Toby wasn't keen to participate in, but halfway through he said, "Mom, I want to do something for the show."

"What?" I asked.

"I want to burp."

I was horrified. Imagine being the mother of that boy, the one who was so rude? A small voice inside of me told me to get over myself. Let go of my prejudices and shame. If Toby wanted to burp, then I'd have to let him burp and let him find out for himself what sort of response it elicited. I smothered my objections, hid my head in shame, and let him go up to the stage. He stood in front of the microphone and let out a burp the size of Canada. The whole crowd burst out laughing. The moderator then shushed them and said, "The camera wasn't working, Toby, can you do that again?" So, he let out another huge rumbling burp right into the microphone. The crowd went crazy, whistling and stamping their feet. For the remainder of the week and on into 2021 when we met up with people from that summit, they didn't remember me, but if I mentioned the burping boy, every single one of them remembered Toby.

I'm not likening holistic healing to burping! I'm just recognizing that very often we have preconceived notions of how certain thoughts and behaviors will be accepted. Also, that a lot of our behavior and expectations are learned from society, but that doesn't always make them right. To be honest, this is a complicated subject and also doesn't always make them wrong. Playing with your penis in the grocery store is still one of the taboos that we prefer to avoid. Toby's going to be so mad at me for including that, but the older I get, the braver I get, and the more I'm willing to deal with the consequences!

Very often in this funny old world of ours, we allow bad things to happen just because we don't want to be seen to be going against popular opinion. I'm thinking here of issues like climate change and pollution. The 'bunny huggers' who fight so hard for a healthy future and world are vilified. The more that happens, the more outrageous their attempts to be noticed and get their issues noticed. I think also of the adults and children who were present when Devan Selvey was murdered. There were many who didn't want to interfere or cause a scene, who are living with a lifetime of regrets now.

Even taking Toby out of conventional schooling was really hard for me. I was so afraid. Afraid of criticism, afraid that he would end up a failure, my failure. My intuition told me it was fine, but my conscious self, framed by society, argued that it was impossible to achieve if we didn't follow the same route as the majority. It took time for me to let go altogether, to let go of public opinion and expectation, and live life according to my heart and my own rules. It wasn't until I'd met a number of young adults, who had learned experientially, and seen that they were intelligent people, who could not only read and write and do mathematics, but had wonderful confidence and knowledge far more extensive than what the classroom can offer, that I had the courage to drop the school curriculum.

That I have been able to recognize and apply my passions as a result of Toby's education is a bonus for me.

Strangely enough, all my wanderings have brought me closer to my parents, and taught us all tolerance. Unfortunately, that is not the case with my brother, but I've come to accept that we are just very different, and we both deserve the peace and space to get on with living our own lives and being ourselves. I am preoccupied by issues of existential meaning; he is preoccupied with the here and the now, with building a comfortable retirement. This is no longer my issue. We each have the right to live our lives the way we want to. I have let him go.

Toby and I will stay digital nomads for the foreseeable future. We hope to leave Mexico for the summer and travel to Guatemala, Nicaragua, or Ecuador where we can continue our Spanish studies. I don't know what will happen after that; it will depend on the world travel situation (and no, I don't have a crystal ball to give me a peek into that). I don't choose what I can see or sense; each vision is a gift for which I am grateful.

I still suffer from migraines, but in general, I cope better. I have rid myself of all the drugs that were prescribed for me after my accident, other than a non-narcotic migraine pill when the migraines are at their worst. I'm not entirely sure how it works, but I'm glad it does. It's made up of enzymes that encourage my brain to produce some sort of neurotransmitter, a lack of which causes the migraines. I don't drink alcohol; I don't smoke, and I no longer use CBD oil. I don't need to; I no longer need crutches that blur my reality. I am okay with the pain of reality, and with the joy of it. I have learned to let that pain go; if you can't, you close yourself to new and exciting experiences. I have also let go of the notion that I need a man in my life. I don't. If I ever meet a like-minded man, who can love me for who and what I am, that'll be wonderful, but it's not a priority; what will be will be.

I haven't found perfect inner peace. I'm not sure that you can be both alive and at peace at all times. I have many interests in life, and I'm not a daydreamer. I care intensely about world issues, and have a very strong sense of justice; these two factors alone will probably always ensure that there is some form of conflict in my life. However, that I can accept and am willing to live with. I am not at peace with the world, there is too much out there for me to make peace with, but I am at peace with myself.

What I have learned is that the meaning of life is simpler than I could ever have imagined. Live life on your terms, do what makes your heart sing—conformity may give you societal acceptance, but it's not guaranteed to make you happy. Living life on your own terms may not always pay the bills, but with balance, it can bring you satisfaction and comfort.

Some of the wisest words I've ever read were penned quite recently, by a surprisingly young woman:

"Your new life is going to cost you your old one. It's going to cost you your comfort zone and your sense of direction.

It's going to cost you relationships and friends. It's going to cost you being liked, and understood.

Because the people who are meant for you are going to meet you on the other side.

And you're going to build a new comfort zone around the things that actually move you forward.

And instead of liked, you're going to be loved.

Instead of understood, you're going to be seen.

All you're going to lose is what was built for a person you no longer are. Let it go."

—Brianna Wiest

References

CNN, B. J. W., for. (2018, May 15). *Underground Budapest: Caverns, churches and Cold War bunkers.* CNN. https://edition.cnn.com/travel/article/budapest-underground/index.html

Elephanta Island | Description & Facts. (1998, July 20). Encyclopedia Britannica. https://www.britannica.com/place/Elephanta-Island

Joanna. (2016, April 13). *Find heaven and hell in Da Nang's Marble Mountains.* The Blond Travels. https://www.theblondtravels.com/marble-mountains-da-nang/

Lake Nasser | lake, Africa. (1998, July 20). Encyclopedia Britannica. https://www.britannica.com/place/Lake-Nasser

Liberti, L. (n.d.). *Project World School.* Project World School. Retrieved March 4, 2021, from https://projectworldschool.com

Planet, L. (n.d.). *Wat Pho in Bangkok, Thailand.* Lonely Planet. Retrieved March 12, 2021, from https://www.lonelyplanet.com/a/nar/3ed16a46-0494-43dc-81c2-59881cf95afb/1324177

The Editors of Encyclopedia Britannica. (2017). Abu Simbel | archaeological site, Egypt. In *Encyclopædia Britannica*. https://www.britannica.com/place/Abu-Simbel

Tierney, A. (n.d.). *Outschool: Take small-group classes, from anywhere*. Outschool. https://Outschool.com

Visit Centro de Ciencias Explora on your trip to Leon or Mexico. (n.d.). Www.inspirock.com. Retrieved March 12, 2021, from https://www.inspirock.com/mexico/leon/centro-de-ciencias-explora-a1364695691

Wiest, B. (2020). *The Mountain is You: Transforming Self-Sabotage into Self-Mastery*. Thought Catalog Books.

Wikipedia Contributors. (2021, March 10). *Lønstrup*. Wikipedia; Wikimedia Foundation. https://en.wikipedia.org/wiki/L%C3%B8nstrup